The Anglo-Saxon Village

Bernice Zieba

Jan Webmedia

Copyright © 2023 Bernice Zieba
All rights reserved.
bernicezieba.com
ISBN: 9798872657835

Published by: Jan Webmedia
First published: 2023

Copy editing: Oxford Editors
Formatting: Jan Webmedia
Cover design: Jan Webmedia

janwebmedia.uk

Contents

Chapter One—Leaving England
Chapter Two—Travelling the World
Chapter Three—Getting Lost
Chapter Four—The Longboat
Chapter Five—Singing Fjords
Chapter Six—The Trolls
Chapter Seven—The Open Sea
Chapter Eight—Life on the Boat
Chapter Nine—Sea Monster
Chapter Ten—Thirst and Hunger
Chapter Eleven—Kraken
Chapter Twelve—Pictland
Chapter Thirteen—Cymry
Chapter Fourteen—St Dewi's
Chapter Fifteen—Dinner with the Monks
Chapter Sixteen—The Monastery
Chapter Seventeen—Back at the Camp
Chapter Eighteen—Back in Mercia
Chapter Nineteen—Hamberton Market
Chapter Twenty—Back at the Friary
Chapter Twenty-One—Back at the Village
Chapter Twenty-Two—Reunion
Chapter Twenty-Three—Revealing the Call
Chapter Twenty-Four—Talk with Bede
Chapter Twenty-Five—Assessment
Chapter Twenty-Six—Another Reunion
Chapter Twenty-Seven—Village Life
Chapter Twenty-Eight—The Wedding
Chapter Twenty-Nine—Attack
Chapter Thirty—At the River Bank
Chapter Thirty-One—Change of Direction
Chapter Thirty-Two—The New Prior
Chapter Thirty-Three—Conclusion

Chapter One – Leaving England

Do you remember that in my last story I told you about my sister and me going to another place, another world? We had many adventures there, and we wished to return. But until now it never happened. In fact, life just went on and we grew old in the meantime. Forty years ago, I got married. But my wife, Veronica, died of cancer when she was fifty. For the past twenty years I have remained a widower and focused on my architectural projects. Many of them, I admit, have stayed uncompleted. But at least they kept me occupied.

It was after our father's death in March (he reached the good age of 96 and passed away only a year after our mum) when Rohanna and I headed out to the house where we had spent most of our youth, and where our parents had lived until the end of their days. The house was up for sale and we had to clear things out and sign some boring documents.

By the way, Rohanna never married. And if you remember my story about the Anglo-Saxon village, you'd understand why. She never spoke about it openly, but Durwyn, whom she met all those years ago, had such an impact on her that any other man who was interested in her had no chance. There wasn't anything wrong with these men, and I don't think Rohanna was being picky. She was simply keeping a secret promise, and nobody and nothing could make her break it. I'm not sure if she was entirely happy, though; but anyway, she decided not to marry and thus she became a spinster. Then when we returned to our childhood home, old memories sprang to life. It was as if the mysterious journey to Mercia, the Anglo-Saxon kingdom, had happened only a short while ago.

We were packing some leftover items of our parents', such as clothes, ornaments, bath towels (all the furniture was already sold), when I remembered something I'd hidden in a wall closet after returning from Mercia as a twelve-year-old.

"I've got to see if it's still there!" I said to Rohanna, thinking of the necklace with the cross. The key to the closet was hanging on a nail just below the ceiling in the left corner when entering the kitchen. (As a child I'd had to stand on a chair to hang it up, but now I just reached out with my hand to take it down.) The tiny closet was built into the wall on the top floor near the loft. It was covered over in the same paint as the wall, and therefore was easily overlooked. It might have originally been a key cupboard, but my family never used it as such. I unlocked its little door, and the scent of wood and varnish sent me back to those childhood years. It smelt exactly the same as when I had hidden the chain necklace away. I carefully took it in my hands: the golden cross with the circle still glistened as it had decades ago. There wasn't even dust in the cupboard.

"It's still here!" I exclaimed.

"It's beautiful," Rohanna answered. "Are you going to wear it after all these years?"

"Later," I said, and slipped it into my trouser pocket.

She sighed, and I knew her thoughts were drifting off to Durwyn; but as usual I avoided mentioning it.

My red Fiat was packed with the leftover items from our parents' house, and we were ready to leave. I locked the front door and felt a pinch in my heart. This was the last time; we would never return to this house. It was hard holding back the tears.

"Oh well," I thought, "this is life. Nothing on earth remains for ever."

But before we opened the car door, Rohanna grabbed my arm and without saying anything nudged me towards the gate to the left of the house that led to the back garden.

"Let's walk down the path one more time ... you know where."

I sighed. "All right, let's do it for the last time, but without any expectations!"

This walk from the back garden down the path behind the fence had become a kind of ritual in the past decades. Since we had moved away from home in our twenties, we'd met at Mum and Dad's occasionally and we'd walk down the path, secretly hoping to hear the chapel bell ring again—the chimes that had brought us to Mercia.

This time I felt awkward, because I knew it was going be the last time. The house would soon be inhabited by other people, and it would become their garden. We wouldn't be able to enter someone else's territory and pass through the gate that leads to the hidden path.

I pressed down the handle of the rusty gate, still the same old one. The back garden was now overgrown with ivy, especially behind the shed which had now been replaced with a new one. Rohanna closed the gate behind her and we walked down the path that led through the little forest. Hardly anything had changed here since we were children, although the rest of the village was full of new houses and shopping centres—you wouldn't recognise it any more.

I knew that I wouldn't hear the ringing of the chapel bell on the hill. But half of me still held onto the idea. Nothing happened, however: not one ding, not one dong, not a sound that could resemble a ringing bell. Rohanna didn't say a word all the way until we reached the foot of the hill. She looked up at the chapel and shrugged her shoulders. And that was it. We didn't go up the hill. Instead, we walked back another way, which led through the village and back to where my car was parked, in front of Mum and Dad's house. There the sign was still standing which said that the house was sold. We slumped in our car seats and drove off.

"You know what this means?" Rohanna asked, breaking her minutes of silence.

"What?" I asked. And then I remembered. "Oh, of course … now is the time for our world trip!" I smiled. Then the memory of my wife came to me. "But first, let's visit Veronica. I promised to let her know when we'd be off," I said and drove towards the parish graveyard.

"Do you think Veronica ever believed our story about Mercia?" Rohanna asked. It wasn't the first time she'd asked that question.

"I don't know for sure," I answered. "But I'm sure she would have loved it as much as we did. She even took notes of my narrative. Perhaps she once wanted to write a story about it, if only she'd had the chance to get there…" I sighed.

Rohanna stayed several steps behind me when I stopped at the gravestone, which had the name Veronica Baker carved in it, and in my mind I said to Veronica:

"Remember the journey Rohanna and I vowed we'd take if the bell never called us back to Mercia? Well, that time has now come. We're going to do it! We're going to travel the world. I can hardly believe it. I'm as excited as a child. Can you imagine me, an old man, going on such an adventure? I know it's crazy. But you loved unusual things, and I'm sure you'd love this too. And I'm taking you with me in my heart, of course! I wish you were here."

I wiped away some tears before I turned around. Then with a meaningful smile I whispered to Rohanna, "Let's go!" And I knew that she knew this didn't simply mean leaving the graveyard. This was to be the beginning of an adventure!

As agreed on before, we had just two days to pack our suitcases and get everything ready; just two days, so that we wouldn't get distracted by our own doubts or anything else that could prevent us from our undertaking—you know, the kind of thoughts that keep people back from achieving their goal or living their dream.

I'm glad we settled on two days, because I couldn't wait for the departure. To be honest, I had already secretly made preparations for this world tour years before—and I'm pretty sure that Rohanna had too.

Our long journey began on the day when Rohanna arrived to pick me up and drive us to the airport; and it was the day I left everything behind. Which wasn't really difficult for me, because my wife, Veronica, and I never had children (although we wished for them). My 19-year-old cat, the last of the series of eleven cats (sometimes I kept two or three at the same time), had passed away last year. And all my well-kept furniture, the paintings and photos on the walls, the hand-painted ceramic plates set up on the country-style cupboard (the way Veronica liked it) and every other thing remained in their place; they had served their purpose, and I wouldn't miss anything. I was ready to leave.

One last glance in the mirror. My grey hair was trimmed short, my glasses were safe in my pocket (I would need them for reading the departure times), my brown eyes looked back at me with a glint, ready for the unknown. I completed my traveller's look with a white straw hat, which I took down from the hook; it was more suited to summer than early spring, but we'd soon be in warmer parts of the globe.

Just before I closed the bright-blue front door, the sun shone in from the kitchen window at the other end of the hall through the stained-glass window—as if to say goodbye. I wondered if I would see my neat little English home (which I had designed myself) ever again.

Chapter Two—Traveling the World, to Norway

I won't go into much detail on our world trip. We did get to see ever such a lot. The world is rich in all kinds of things, many of which I didn't even know existed. Everything seemed to go well (apart from a few flight delays, the occasional shaky road journey or a train apartment filled with smoke where you couldn't open the windows to let in fresh air); but overall it was a happy journey. We went on safari in Kenya, visited the jungle in Burma, travelled on the Trans-Siberian Railway to Novosibirsk, which lasted eight days, tasted sushi in Japan, met kangaroos and koala bears in Australia, before we finally flew to Norway. Five months of globetrotting had passed. We had touched down on every continent except for the Americas and Antarctica.

But then Rohanna said she'd become tired of travelling the world and maybe it was time to go back home, to England. She had come to the conclusion that it wasn't worth escaping the shadows of the past. "We have to put up with our lives as they are," she said.

"And face the fact that our life is here and now, and we needn't dig around in the past any more?" I asked, and she nodded in agreement.

By then it was late August: there'd be plenty to do in my garden at home and I had enough books to read as the weather got cooler and the days shorter. So I didn't counter the idea of returning home.

In Norway, we spent the last days of our world trip in a small hotel in a little town on a narrow fjord, surrounded by mountains that led down to the sea.

There was a Viking museum nearby, and we thought it was worth a visit.

Once there, something struck me from inside. It wasn't the exhibition itself (displaying Viking finds and replicas, bones, ancient jewellery, straw huts and long ships), but a sudden and intense memory of Mercia, together with a strong longing to be there.

Throughout our life, we had often thought of this other world where we had spent five days of our childhood, but it was a distant memory, a faint impression from the past, and it became fainter over the years. While staring at a reconstruction of Viking people (models dressed up and sitting around a fireplace—a flickering electric simulation—holding wooden bowls, surrounded by walls made of twigs, mud and straw, and a thatched roof), I remembered the Anglo-Saxon village. The flashback was unusually intense. It was as if I were there, as if I could just reach out with my hand and touch it, as if I could smell the leather, the furs, the smoke, the cooking. In my mind, the figures in front of me sprang to life. I heard the voices of the villagers and I saw myself sitting at the fireplace in Durwyn's hut.

"Of course," I thought to myself, "this is just my brain playing tricks on me. Those are just impressions that have been stored away for a long time and are now triggered by what I see in this museum."

Yet I stood a little longer, staring at the scene and pondering the flashback. I didn't mention it to Rohanna because, although we often have similar thoughts, I didn't want to confuse her in case she didn't experience the same.

"There's a film running over there," I said, pointing to a corner where a half-drawn black curtain revealed a screen on the wall. We sat down in the plastic chairs and watched a documentary about Viking invasions. The continuous narration made me sleepy, and I fell into a doze while the fiercest battles were taking place on screen. I didn't wake until Rohanna nudged me saying, "Come on, Adrian, it's almost five. They're closing soon, and we still need to find out what time our ship is leaving in the morning."

Chapter Three – Getting Lost

Our plan was to travel from this small town to Bergen, from where we'd take the ferry to England. But first we needed to go down to the port to check ferry times. We left the museum, went to our hotel rooms, changed into long-sleeved clothes (August evenings were cool in Norway), grabbed our essentials (we always carried our passport, money and other important things in a shoulder bag) and headed on foot down the asphalt mountain road to the shore. It should only have been a twenty-minute walk to the little port, but then something happened that we hadn't expected.

Suddenly, from out of nowhere, fog rose up and wrapped itself around us. It became so thick that we could hardly see one another, even though we were walking close to each other. It was all grey and white and moist; we couldn't recognise where we were going, nor anything around us. The mountain slopes, the grassy patches, the rocks, the sky had all vanished—we could have been anywhere, because nothing was visible. The only thing I was still aware of was the hard asphalt road under my feet. I didn't see it, I just felt it with every step as we cautiously carried on walking down the road. The fog was made up of teeny water drops which stuck to my face and hands and chilled my whole body. I wished I had a raincoat, but we had left our anoraks in the hotel room, along with our suitcases. I wiped the water droplets from my hair, and then I realised that the ground was no longer asphalt.

Instead of the "thud, thud" under our feet there was a "crunch, crunch".

"We're walking on gravel," I stated.

"Yes, it's some sort of natural path," Rohanna answered as she slipped her arm through mine. We kept on walking at a slow pace. With all the rocks and steep slopes nearby, and without seeing where we were going, we had to be careful. We had tried to stick to the road, but now there didn't seem to be a road any more. And we weren't sure whether we were going in the right direction.

"Weren't we silly to leave the hotel at this time of the evening? We could at least have asked one of the locals to show us the way," I said with a sigh.

"Yes, it was rather foolish of us," Rohanna agreed.

"We've travelled to so many different parts of the world, but nothing ever happened to us. And now, in this modern and organised country, we're lost in the fog on a risky mountain road!"

"Well, I don't think this is still a road. I'm sure a car couldn't drive here," Rohanna answered. The surface had degenerated from gravel to grass. We must have been following a narrow footpath. As we carried on step by step, the fog still remained thick. We might have been out for over an hour now, and darkness was closing in.

Then we heard a distant flowing, rushing sound: not very loud, but rather calm and regular. It was the sound of a river.

"The gravel has given out," Rohanna announced. "We're now walking on rocks with patches of sand."

"We must be near the shore!"

I also noticed something else. "Your voice is sounding so soft," I said, wondering if it was due to the moisture in the air. I wiped more droplets from my face and then noticed that I could now see my hand quite clearly, even though I wasn't wearing my reading glasses.

"Why am I seeing everything so clearly?" I asked, thinking aloud.

"It's probably because in this fog we can't see anything at all," Rohanna mocked.

"No, I don't mean the things we can't see. But I can see my hands in front of me more clearly than usual."

I also noticed that my backache had gone. I usually got muscle pain from walking downhill. "This Norwegian air must be good for us," I mumbled. But there wasn't time to discuss it, because at that moment we heard voices. As the voices came closer, we could tell that people were shouting to each other in what first sounded like a strangely accented Norwegian. But I soon realised that I was able to understand every word.

There was also an orange spot of light that moved around jerkily. The fog was now disappearing and soon I recognised that the orange light was coming from the flame of a torch. It was held by a bearded man, shining it in our faces and making everything around us appear orange-red. Rohanna's hair (which was grey) now looked red; in fact, it looked like the hair colour she'd had when she was young.

The bearded man with the torch examined us. "Ah, there ye are at last, by Odin!" he cried out. He turned around, directing the fire-torch ahead, and beckoned us to follow. So we marched behind him, and after a few yards we arrived at the water.

"We need to leave as long as the wind is fortunate. Now hurry up, ye two, jump onto the ship!" he said, ushering us forwards. "We almost left without ye. By Odin, these young folk…!" he continued, shaking his head.

I didn't understand why he called us "young". Perhaps it was either to flatter or to insult us. I found it odd that he seemed to have expected us, but his appearance was strange too: he was wearing a long tunic and leather shoes like slippers, his long, brown-greyish hair tied back in a ponytail and his beard plaited in two neat braids, tied with string at the end.

Chapter Four—The Longboat

"Ship? What ship?" Rohanna asked puzzled.

"We only came to find out when our ship is leaving," I explained to the bearded man. "We intend to leave tomorrow morning—not now…"

"Ye must be kidding! Tomorrow morning? Today is the day we leave, boy! Only a fool would miss the advantage of this good weather and wind. And besides that, we don't want to attract more attention than necessary, do we? The quicker we get out of 'ere, the better!"

The bearded man stomped a few metres ahead, and as we approached the ship, which I thought looked more like a large wooden boat with a mast, he shouted a couple of orders to a young man, also with a plaited beard. There were two more young men winding up ropes, walking up and down the long wooden boat, preparing the mast. A middle-aged woman was standing in front of the boat, her fists dug in her hips, observing us as we approached.

"About time…" she muttered.

"Wife, have ye got the clothes ready for them?" the man who brought us here shouted.

"Course I have," she answered, still staring at us. "The messenger was right, ye are dressed up weird, with clothes as thin as underwear!" She shook her head disapprovingly. "Ye gotta wear something proper for a journey like this if ye don't wanna freeze your bottoms off!"

The bearded man chuckled. "Yeah, Hearty. When him said: 'Don't wonder if they're dressed differently, just have something ready for 'em to wear', I thought 'more weirdos on board?' Ain't it enough with 'em three young lads without a wife, old Ragnar, and the little lad driving everyone crazy?"

"And now, let's not ask who's the weirdest of 'em all…" his wife said, unimpressed.

"Ye ain't saying that's me, are ye, Hearty?"

"Nay, I ain't saying it, I'm just thinking it!"

"Ain't she cheeky!" he said to the old man sitting in the boat. "But that's how I like 'er."

"The mystery of love!" sang the old man, grinning.

"At least we're complete now, and can finally leave!" the bearded man bellowed.

"But…" Rohanna began, intending to explain that we hadn't booked a ship for tonight. Yet something stopped her. Perhaps it was clear that there was no point in arguing about it. These people had expected us—yes, precisely us, there were no doubts about that. Within a few seconds we had to decide whether this was all destined to be, or whether we should escape from these strangers as quickly as possible.

"What do you think?" I whispered to Rohanna. "Shall we risk it?"

"I can't say. It all seems so natural for them. But they are a bunch of strange people … and this was not in our plan! We've also left our suitcases in the hotel room!"

There were more people in the boat: a young blonde woman with a baby in her arms, and a little boy, about five years old, running around, climbing over baskets and bundles, tapping the knees of a man who seemed to be his dad. The little boy kept asking the young mother, "When are we leaving, when, Mama?"

"Just sit down now, Olfi," she answered. "We're going to leave any moment! Stop asking, I've told you so many times!"

I almost felt guilty for standing around and causing more delay to the departure.

"Shall we just join them?" Rohanna whispered, and it seemed she was more inclined to step into the boat than not to.

"At least we took our passports and some money with us," I whispered back. In just two steps we were over the edge and into the boat. But then we understood that something mysterious, something unexplainable, was happening.

"Do you think…?" Rohanna began to ask.

But before she could finish her sentence, I answered,

"Yes, I think so…!"

What we both meant, but didn't say aloud, was that we both knew we had been transported once again into another world, and there was no way we could run away from it.

There were several rows of benches and the elderly man pointed to one of them in the middle of the boat, where I spotted two piles of neatly folded clothes. The young mother saw us looking at them and nodded: "Helga says those are now yers to wear."

I unfolded a tunica and a leather belt, and there was a long thick dress for Rohanna. There were also two long cloaks, which didn't seem necessary at the moment. I threw the tunica over my thin sweater, and Rohanna pulled the dress over her dotted summer blouse. The material felt rough, probably linen, but it was loose enough to wear comfortably on top of our own light summer clothes. The tunica reached down to my knees, and I exchanged my own trousers for a pair of brown, baggy trousers.

I felt unusual in these clothes, but I was glad of them, because as soon as we had stepped onto the boat it was fresher than on land, and I knew it would get colder. The thick material would keep us warm. There was a lot of baggage stacked around us (sacks, baskets and wooden boxes—also cages with hens and even a goat), and as soon as we were all aboard, the men and Helga all grabbed an oar. Someone started calling "Heave ho!" and the others joined in while the boat began to move. Then all seven paddlers kept repeating "Heave ho!" until their calls turned into song and the boat moved swiftly over the water. The men chanted in low voices, sounding like the constant beat of a drum or the grumbling sound of a bass tuba or both together; meanwhile the women, with their higher voices, began to sing a song about sailing into the wide and unknown world, not loudly, as if they didn't want to disturb the peaceful night.

A torch was burning to light up the boat. In this dim light, I observed the travellers around us. Two of the young men were blond, and another had dark hair. The young mother's baby was now asleep, covered with a woollen blanket in a basket padded with animal skin. The little boy gazed over the edge of the boat, his arm hanging over the rim, watching how the world moved by.

Regular strokes of the oars moved the boat smoothly down the fjord. Someone put out the torch and darkness fell upon us. In the black sky, the half moon shone brightly, surrounded by twinkling stars. The moonlight reflected on the water, rippling from the paddle strokes. One of the men stood up and pulled on the ropes connected to the masts. I watched the sail slowly unfold. It was a large, white square cloth with a pattern in the centre. As the wind caught in the sail, it took the shape of an enormous half-balloon. The force of the wind pushing against the sail moved the boat more speedily, so the men let go of their oars, except for the elderly man in the back who steered the boat.

Now the singing carried on, but accompanied by a large drum which the bearded man, who had brought us here, beat with a padded stick. It was a flat, wide drum with a low sound. Someone else pulled out a stringed instrument and someone a flute, and they sang and played music for quite a long time. The melody lulled the little boy to sleep, as the music gradually turned quieter and softer. Then instead of singing, there was just humming.

And when the instruments stopped playing there was one humming voice left, until that stopped too.

The boat sailed on gently, pushed by the breeze. The travellers spread out animal furs between the rowing benches; some might be falling asleep, but others, like me, were still gazing at the sky's scattering of thousands of stars and watching the dark mountain silhouettes pass by like enormous giants guarding over the river. I wondered where the journey was leading, and although we were among complete strangers, there was something deep inside which made me trust them. With these strange feelings, I drifted off to sleep.

Chapter Five—Singing Fjords

When I awoke, it was still dark. The fur on which I had been sleeping was surprisingly comfortable. I had covered myself with the hooded cloak, which proved to be as warm as a blanket. What had woken me was once again music, or rather a peculiar singing, but it didn't come from my fellow travellers. Mellow, but loud voices were sounding back and forth across the fjord, as if the mountains towering above the banks were calling to each other. And I think they were! The melodic shouts resounded like call and response in an empty cathedral. Occasionally there was the pluck of a stringed instrument, bouncing back between the cliffs; and sometimes there was the sound of a deep horn, like the hoot of a steam boat, but longer and softer. There was something cool and refreshing in the sound of this strange music—like newly fallen snow, and also soft and delightful, like an endless bed of flowers. Mountains from one side of the fjord called out a question, and the mountains on the other side echoed back. Sometimes the melodic calls came from both sides simultaneously. All the while the boat drifted gently downstream, hardly making a sound.

In the meantime Rohanna was awake too. "What is this beautiful singing?" she whispered. "Are the mountains making this sound?"

I was not the only one to be woken by this strange music.

"Who's that still a-singing?" the wire-haired young man asked with a sleepy voice.

"Karl, that ain't none of us singing," said one of the blond men. "Just listen, those ain't people's voices!"

"What's all this?" the other blond man asked, sitting up and rubbing his eyes.

Helga was awake too. "That ain't no human voice, I'm telling ye. That must be…" and then the old man, who didn't seem to have slept at all, or if he did, he had nodded off while sitting at the steering oar, completed her sentence: "…The Singing of the Fjord!"

"The Singing of the Fjord!" Helga repeated in awe.

"Ye only get to hear this once in a lifetime!" the old man said.

Helga nudged her husband, who was still snoring next to her. "Wake up, Bard, ye can't miss this!"

Bard turned over to carry on sleeping, but then shot up, suddenly aware of the singing. He brushed his hair back with his hand. "By Odin," he said, "what's this? I hear music! And what music indeed!"

"Yes, it's The Singing of the Fjord, Ragnar says," Helga explained.

"I'm telling ye, ye only get to hear this once in a lifetime," Ragnar repeated, "and that's only if yer lucky. And we are lucky!"

"Well I never!" said Bard, gazing at the mountains in amazement.

The mountains, partly illuminated by the half moon, seemed now higher than hours ago, when we had left. The fjord had become narrower, but it was still wide enough for our craft to pass through without hitting the rocks.

"Beware when the music is over," Ragnar suddenly said, after we had listened for some time.

"What's that you're saying?" asked Bard.

"Beware, when it's all over," Ragnar repeated.

"What then?" Helga asked. "Do you mean the trolls?"

"Yes, they're bound to be out and about. That singing—yes, it's a beauty—but it also wakes up them trolls. We'll see, we'll see…"

"Them trolls!" Helga nodded. "They're bound to come out. I've heard of it. Oh, let's hope they leave us in peace."

"What's that you've heard about them trolls, Helga?" Bard asked.

"Oh, them trolls are not so good. Well, let's wait and see."

As the music waned, the younger men pulled their hoods up again and rolled back into a comfortable position to sleep. I too snuggled in with the soft melody still going on in my head. The gentle rocking of the boat smacking the water against the wooden planks on the sides of the boat lulled me back to sleep. But this was one of those long nights when sleep gets interrupted more than once.

Chapter Six—The Trolls

"Ho, ho! Halt, who comes there?" A male, high-pitched voice was shouting and waking us up. The boat was inching through the narrowest part of the fjord. To both sides the cliffs were only an oar's length away. Several figures with fire torches in their hands loomed up on a bridge—not a man-made bridge, but a natural bridge made of mountain rock forming an arch over the water. Ragnar steered the boat with care, concentrating on not running the boat into the rocks.

"Halt, halt, haaalt!" the voice called again from the middle of the rock bridge. In the light of the torch flame, I saw a short male figure. A pair of dark mocking eyes glinted as he stared at our boat. His face was short and wide, as if it had been pressed together. He had short legs and large ears and his hair was dark-ginger, sticking up in stiff ends. He wore striped baggy trousers and a tunic girded by a thick leather belt in which he stuck one of his hands.

Ragnar and Bard steered to the river bank and with the help of a long pole (the water must have been quite shallow at this point) brought the boat to a halt. Immediately, around six or seven of these figures gathered at the boat. They were armed with spears and swords, stuck in their sides. The one who had demanded us to halt jumped into our boat, holding his spear as if ready to use.

"Now, what's all this about, Troll?" Ragnar asked.

"Oh, oh, oh!" exclaimed the Troll, examining the travellers. "Who have we here, and what's the reason?"

"What's the reason?" Bard repeated. "Well, it should be obvious—we're travelling. Or at least we would be if we weren't disturbed by ye Trolls."

The Troll pointed with his spear to Bard. "So, you're the leader, I guess?"

"Call me that, if it pleases you."

The Troll did a tour of the boat, observing each face like at a border passport control. Was he going to demand proof of my identity? Sleepy as I was, I might have unwittingly pulled out my passport from the little bundle and showed it. Then pointing with his spear at each of us, the Troll counted: "One, two, three, four, five, six, seven, eight, nine ... ten." When he discovered the two children asleep, he slowed down with counting, "eleeeven, tweeelve…"

"Two little humans as well?" he said, stepping closer to examine the two infants in the light of his torch.

The young mother shielded their faces with her hands.

"Keep the light off 'em!" she said, annoyed.

The young father stood up, putting himself between the children and the Troll.

"They're asleep," he said with a quiver in his voice, blocking off the Troll. "If them wakes up, they're gonna not stop screaming!"

Bard came closer too. "Don't even think of it…" he growled at the Troll.

After staring at the children, the Troll suddenly moved on. "Na, na, na, too much trouble, these little human creatures. Too much trouble!" he said brushing the air with his hand. The young parents remained quiet, watching the Troll move on.

"What's all this?" the little figure then asked, pointing with his spear at the bundles and boxes. The hens in the cages slept, just letting out an occasional "cluck". The goat lay on the ground, its ears waggling, bleating quietly while half asleep.

"All ours," Bard said, as the Troll poked the luggage with the spear tip. "Nothing of value for a Troll, nothing whatsoever! No gold, no jewels, nothing precious—just clothes and household stuff."

The Troll waved to one of his companions, who instantly obeyed.

"Yes, Master Garon?"

"Unpack!"

The other Troll began unfolding the bundles and opening boxes. He dug around with his hands in the items, but didn't find anything his master found worthy of his attention.

Suddenly, Garon pointed his spear at two small bundles. Obeying Garon's orders, the other Troll grabbed the bundles. As he unfolded the clothes, our shoulder bags with the passports and purses rolled out, and this caught the attention of Garon who snatched them up.

"Ah, what's this? What's this?" Garon asked, looking through the contents of my purse. There were some coins and a few bank cards in there. Then he did the same with Rohanna's purse, and browsed through the passports with a puzzled look on his face.

"Will do, will do!" he exclaimed, and the other Troll hastily took our things and dropped them in a sack which he carried on his back.

Rohanna and I both watched with dismay: the Trolls had confiscated our possessions! Rohanna sat bolt upright and shifted with her feet, ready to protest.

Bard moved close to us. "Let 'em have it. We can be glad if that's all they takes…" he muttered under his breath, just loud enough for Rohanna and me to hear.

Of course it was better that the Trolls took our passports and purses rather than kidnap the children and take our food. We could do without passports and money, because if we had slipped into the past—and that's what had happened—we wouldn't need them any more.

Then the "border control" search was over and both Trolls skipped off the boat. Standing on the river bank, they waved and shouted: "Off, then! Off you go!"

Ragnar took hold of the stirring oar and the other men with Helga each took up their paddle and we sailed away into the dark.

"Could've been worse," Bard said, when we were out of earshot of the Trolls.

"Ha, and luckily," Bard said, "they didn't discover our trading goods!"

"Yes, all well hidden—thanks be," Helga said, knocking with her fist on the bench on which she sat. The bench was covered with boards on all sides, like a chest.

"This is where you should keep your valuables!" she said, pointing down to the bench where we sat. The others agreed, and it appeared that we had been the only ones who didn't know of the hiding places. But it was too late now. There was nothing left to hide away.

"Oh, yes, them Trolls aren't good, but also ain't very bright," she added with a chuckle. "We've been lucky, sure. I've heard of people meeting the Trolls and having a lot more taken!"

"Why do they allow themselves this?" Rohanna asked.

"Ah, them Trolls own this area, you see. They are controlling their land: who comes in or out has to pay. But you don't always bump into 'em. It's just a matter of fate, really."

After leaving the rock bridge, the fjord remained quite narrow for a while. Then it grew wider, until the shore on both sides was a hundred metres away from the boat, then five hundred, and eventually we found ourselves in the open sea. By then the oarsmen had stopped rowing, and everyone had fallen asleep once again.

Chapter Seven—The Open Sea

When I woke again, the sun was already up, shining warm on my face. Mist rose from the sea, but soon evaporated because of the sun beams. It might have been around ten o'clock in the morning. Most of the passengers slept late after all that had happened last night.

One of the first things that startled me that morning was when I discovered that I had slept next to a young red-haired girl. I observed her from the side—she was sitting and gazing at the water that stretched all around us. The mountains of the fjord were still visible in the east where the sun was rising, but they were now far away.

For a few seconds I wondered who this young girl was, because I couldn't remember any female persons other than the mother with the two children and Helga. When the girl turned round, my eyes widened. The girl stared back at me and slapped her hand over her mouth, suppressing a scream of surprise. During the night we hadn't seen each other well because of the dark. Now, in the bright daylight, everything was revealed, including details and colours that had been covered before by the darkness of night. The girl, of course, was Rohanna; only now she was young again! She wore her hair tied up, like the day before, but her hair was dark red, her face smooth without wrinkles, and from her eyes shone the liveliness of youth. Her hands didn't belong to a seventy-year-old; they were slim and smooth.

"Is it possible?" I asked. "You're young again!"

"And you? You too! Look at you! Your hair is brown again, and you have no wrinkles! You look like ... a sixteen- or seventeen-year-old!" She couldn't help giggling, while I shook my head in disbelief. I wanted to see myself in a mirror, but of course we were now at sea and our fellow travellers wouldn't even know what a mirror was. I leaned over the edge of the boat, trying to catch a glimpse of my reflection. The water was rippling, but looking back at me from the reflection was a familiar-looking face. Now I remembered why Rohanna's hair had looked red in the light of the torch yesterday night, why her voice had changed and why my health was restored (my back pains had vanished, my eyes could see well). Now it made sense, why Bard had called us "young folk"!

Just then I became aware that Bard had been watching us. "Well, didn't I say so: weirdos!" he muttered to his wife Helga.

"Come on, let's sit down for breakfast!" she said, not paying attention to his comment.

"Is there enough for everyone?" Rohanna asked, with an apologetic tone in her voice. "We haven't brought anything with us, I'm sorry!"

"Sorry?" Helga laughed. "There's plenty! There's enough on board for a whole warrior troop!"

"Yes, come and sit down. Ye must be hungry," Bard said. He poked his finger in my chest and added, "Ye'll need a good feed, because yer gonna be rowing today, and ye look like yer been sitting lots, not doing much bodily work at all!"

When I looked at the other three young men and Bard, and also old Ragnar, I had to admit that they all looked strongly built and fit. They must have been used to hard work, unlike me, who spent so much time sitting at a desk, writing and planning, or sitting in a comfortable armchair reading books.

As the others rose from their resting places, splashing cool seawater on their faces, Helga and the young mother began unpacking dried, salted meat and flat bread. There was drinking water in leather bottles, and someone had milked the goat and carried a small bucket of goat's milk to where everyone was gathered in the middle of the boat, seated on benches, sacks and boxes.

"We've a-heard yer from the land of Angles, and we were told that ye'll show us where we can settle! You know, we're off to Mercia, the green and pleasant land. And not to raid, just to settle!" Bard began.

"Tell us about yerself," Helga said. "Are ye two a couple who wanted to get married and weren't allowed to?" she asked while throwing pieces of flat bread over to Rohanna and me.

"No, no, not at all!" Rohanna replied, suppressing a chuckle.

"We're brother and sister," I said. "We're twins. We're not escaping. No, we're ... well we're on a journey back home to Engl... I mean, to Mercia."

"Ah, I see. Well, I say, twins!"

"Ha, twins! That brings bad luck, doesn't it?" said Bard.

"Or good luck," said Helga.

"Whichever—it comes in double," Ragnar said, pouring water into mugs and handing them round.

"Never mind," Bard added, "it won't be hard to find a man for the maiden—there's enough young men who will like 'er pretty looks," he said, patting the two young men's backs who were sitting left and right of him, so that they almost spilt their drink.

"So, yer on your way back to Mercia? That explains yer unusual accent. But I'd say yer fluent in the Norse language ... ye must have spent quite some time among us Norse people!"

At this point I didn't know what to say. Why Rohanna and I were speaking in their language as fluently as in English was another mystery. We just spoke naturally in what we believed was our own language, and somehow they understood. This was as much of a mystery as us turning young again. Then I asked them why *they* were on this journey to the place that Rohanna and I were used to calling England.

"The reason why we want to go to the Land of the Angles is 'cause we want better land," Bard began.

"Is Norway not good enough?" I asked.

"It's harsh in winter, and in the mountainous area where we've lived, it's hard to plough and difficult to grow crops. We've heard of the lush grass and soft earth on your island. It had better be so! And I'm sure it is…"

"You see, we don't wanna raid. We ain't that kind of people! We just wanna lead a normal life and feed our families," Helga said.

"Yeah, we don't wanna fight to gain land (but we're always ready to fight if we 'ave to defend our lives). We're off on this voyage to seek a better life, not to destroy others. In the Land of the Angles, or more exactly in Mercia, I've heard it's warmer than where we come from, which means winter won't be as tough. Why go through another deadly winter of ice and snow and little to no food, when we could 'ave it better? Hmm?"

As soon as Helga mentioned the word "raid", I realised that these people must be Vikings! I knew from history that the Vikings were fearless warriors who used to go on terrible raids, and I was glad to hear that at least these fellow travellers had no such intentions.

"Do you know other people of your folk that *do* go on raids to Mercia?" I asked.

"Ha! Of course! Not far from where we come from, a warrior leader is gathering a troop for an attack. You see, he planned to leave during these last days of summer. We didn't want to join 'em. My young lad, you're an Angle, but you need to know that they are gathering all our young men for the next attack on yer people. And they also wanted to take our own lads! But we weren't 'aving it. Helga's a wise woman and says she: 'Nay, not our sons—

over me dead body!' And ain't she right? So, my family, that's me, me wife Helga, our two sons, we thought we'd get a few people together whom we can trust and go on this journey. So, as ye see, we ended up with this bunch of people." He turned to the old man and carried on: "Here's Ragnar. He's old but adventurous, and full of valuable experience.Then there's this young family," he said, pointing to the blonde mother and the man next to her, who nodded in a friendly manner.

He then presented the young man with dark, curly hair. "This is Karl. He's as good as our own son." Not only was his hair darker than the other Vikings', but also his skin colour. In fact, he looked as if he was partly African, which puzzled me.

"Yer wondering about Karl?" Bard asked and then continued: "It's 'cause Loki came from Asgard to play tricks on him. Loki smoked his hair with a flame, eh, which made his skin dark at the same time," Bard said, smirking.

"Ah, stop being rude," Helga snapped.

"Just kidding, ain't I!" Bard answered. "Ye never get to see brown skin in Norse land. Only in distant countries, far, far south, where only a few Norse have set foot…"

"Do ye mind, Karl, if I tell them about yer background?" Helga asked.

Karl smiled while chewing flat bread, shrugged his shoulders and said: "Go ahead!"

"Well, it's a long story. As Bard said, he's just like our own son. Our two boys," she said with a nod directed towards the two fair-haired young men, "they grew up with him—we've always been neighbours. Karl's mum was a fine girl, she was. But a somewhat adventurous one, weren't she? She went on one of them long journeys with the men. They'd been away longer than twelve months, and when she came back, her belly was large under her dress. She didn't wanna tell anyone what happened, not even trusted friends, who I was one of. We pressed her, trying to get the tale out of her. But she's as stubborn as a stump. We knew about them travellers going on a long adventurous voyage, down south where the weather never gets cold and it's hot all year. Them voyagers been a-trading, met all kinds of folk, and seen so much wondrous things, it makes you jealous." Helga passed on some goat's milk in a jug.

"Ragnar could tell a lot. He's been on countless voyages and seen folk even darker than Karl when travelling to the Egypt-land. There are folks a-trading at market with skin as dark as coal, innit, Ragnar?" Ragnar nodded with his mouth full of bread and cheese.

"Karl's mother was a good one," Helga continued, "but she didn't live long. When Karli was born, we all commented on his dark skin and black hair. But she'd just smile and stroke his tiny head. She was proud of her little one. When some dumb folks said something nasty, while she was still resting after birth, she'd give back: 'Anyone being bad to my Karli gets to know me fists,' and no one dared to make a nasty comment any more. Then when she got hit hard by a cow's hoof on the head, she died not long after, and that's when Karli was only three years old. He grew up with his aunt and uncle, our neighbours—and our boys and him been always playing and fighting together. Can't really imagine life without our Karli, innit, Bard?" she asked and Bard nodded approvingly.

Chapter Eight—Life on the Boat

When we'd finished eating and drinking, Bard got up and said, "Ragnar, how's it? Think we should all be a-rowing, right?"

"Yes, for sure!" Ragnar called back. He pointed at the sun and said, "We need a strong push westwards!" He took up the same place as he'd been the day before, in the back of the boat, and grabbed the steering paddle with his mighty hands.

"Ragnar is our trusted seaman," Bard said. "He knows which direction to go by observing the sun at day, and at night the stars. He knows every star in the sky; in fact, he's so good at navigating that he could find his way even when the stars are covered by clouds." I tried to work out how that goes, while the others just laughed. Bard gave me a strong pat on the back and said, "Up, young lad. Time for you to have your go. Ever been a rower before?"

I couldn't remember ever rowing a boat like this. "No," I said, shaking my head regretfully. I may have paddled a small rubber boat in the past, but that wasn't really worth mentioning. I got up, and remembered that I was young again. That thought strengthened and refreshed me. While Rohanna was still talking with Helga and the young mother (who was washing cloth-nappies in the sea water by leaning over the edge of the boat), I took hold of the long, heavy wooden oar and watched one of Bard's sons in front of me. He pulled on the oar, let it rest for two seconds, then dug into the water and pulled the oar up again while his arm-muscles tensed and his upper body-half leaned to the back. I copied his repeating movements, as well as I could, and soon realised how tough rowing was. I may have been young and fit, but this job required the strength of an athlete. Three men were now rowing on one side of the boat, and three on the other, but there was space for six rowers on each side. Sometimes I had seen Ragnar and Helga rowing too, and now I wondered how even they could row with ease.

After a few minutes the rowers took up their singing again, like the night before. This helped me to forget how heavy the oar was and the strength it needed to push through the water. Today they sang louder than the night before when travelling along the fjord. Now in the open sea, far from land and settlements, no one else could hear us; there was nothing but water and water, all around. The song was the sound of free men. At first I joined in the melody by humming, until bit by bit I learned to sing the words too. The women took out their instruments—drum, flute and string instruments—and played and sang along with us. Someone placed a drum in Rohanna's arms, and it didn't take long for her to join in the catching melody. The little boy bobbed up and down to the rhythm of the music, and took turns with sitting next to a rower and holding onto the oar. He'd soon learn to master rowing too.

We'd been rowing for about half an hour, with short breaks in between for regaining strength, when Ragnar called, "Bjorn, Erik, pull up the sail!" Both brothers got up and grabbed the ropes attached to the sail.

"Heave ho!" Bjorn shouted, and up went the sail like a flag of glory. The large beige cloth with the red pattern in the middle flapped madly while being pulled up, then puffed out presenting its full size. The rowing was over and I was glad to leave the bench to stretch my arms and legs. I was going to have muscle pain after this.

It was now around midday; the sun was burning down on us, while a cool breeze kept us fresh.

Just as I wondered, what we were going to do for the rest of the day, Erik beckoned me to join him, Bjorn and Karl who were sitting on boxes around a board game.

"Can ye play Hnefatafl?" he asked, as I sat down in front of the board.

"It looks like chess," I mumbled, observing the creme-coloured ivory squares and the black and white figures on the board. It was similar to chess but without black and white. Some squares in the centre, on the sides and in each corner were decorated with black swirling patterns. The figures consisted of a king and several warriors.

Erik explained the rules to me. The king was to move first and the way you won was by trapping the king. All pieces on the board moved in straight lines, like the rook in chess. We played always two together, and switched when one game was over. The others easily beat me at first, but after playing a couple of rounds, I was more confident. Sometimes during the game it got loud and tense, occasionally one of them shot up and raised a fist in anger.

"Why are you getting so crazy about it?" I asked trying to calm them down. We had been playing for about two hours.

"Ye call this crazy?" Bjorn laughed out. He pushing his game pieces aside. "Ye know, how warriors drink themselves into a craze, before attacking? Ever experienced that, eh?"

"No, I've never been in a battle" I said, shaking my head.

Bjorn bent over the Hnefatafl board, so he was closer to me, and lowered his voice.

"When them warriors go on their raids, they scream madly, and run and slaughter everything that gets in their way!"

"Why do they do that?" I asked.

"'Cause they aren't just like mad, they actually turn mad! It's the poison they put in their mead before battle.

Drinking the drugged mead makes them brave, but their mind becomes twisted. They don't act like humans anymore, they become monsters!"

"Have no raids taken place in the area from where ye come from?" Karl asked.

"No," I answered, but hesitated. I remembered from history, that raids occurred all across Britain. Who knows, there could have been Viking attacks in the area where I lived.

"Well, ye can be glad if ye never been attacked that way!" Bjorn said.

"I don't see the point of it," Erik added turning a king figure in has hand and examining it. "So much blood and violence. That's why we're travelling to Mercia on our own accord. Before we left, they were planning a new raid and gathered men of our age and above."

"When will the raid take place?" I asked. Bard who had joined us after adjusting the ropes of the sails, and sat down at the game.

"Usually they leave in spring, but this time they were preparing for an autumn raid" he said. "As soon as they have everyone together who they need—around 400 well-trained men—and when the weather and wind is right, they will journey off. We wanted to leave before them. And we had to leave secretly. We didn't want them to know or else, they'd call us cowards and other insults, or they'd persuade our sons to take part in the raid."

"I understand," I said. Now it made sense, why Bard had hurried us onto the boat, and why we had left at night.

"Why should we take part in brutal attacks?" Bjorn continued. "After a raid we'd just be hated by the people in the Land of Angles. And why should peoples hate each other? As you see: ye're an Angle, we're Norse—and we get along well," Bjorn added.

"Yeah, we can even play Hnefatafl without beating each other up," Erik said, and they laughed.

Erik was the younger of the two brothers. He had a long plait while the hair on the sides of his head was shaved to the skin. Bjorn's hair was dark-blond with a tint of red and instead of a plait he wore a short pony tail on one side of his head, while on the other side his hair was cut short. Their beards were plaited too, like Bard's, but not as thick. I estimated that Karl, Erik and Bjorn were 20 years old and above.

When I was finished playing with Karl, Bjorn and Erik, I looked forward to doing something else, but just then Olfi, the little boy (whose proper name was Olaf), came up to me and said: "Now, have a game with me please!" And so, I was stuck with this chess-like game for another half an hour.

All the while, the sail was up pushing the boat forward by itself. Sometimes Ragnar steered the back oar, securing that the boat was heading in the right direction. Ragnar was short and slim, but at the same time he appeared to be strong and swift. His arm muscles must have been trained from decades of field work, rowing and possibly fighting.

In the late afternoon, we had another meal consisting of flat bread (which was now dry and hard), some boiled eggs which they had cooked before departure (according to Helga—the hens were also laying eggs on the boat, but those were put away for trading), more dried meat (which I found out was deer), some dried blue berries and water to drink.

When we were all fed Ragnar then spoke about his trading voyages to the South, how they met all sorts of folk with different shades of skin colour, wearing strange fashions and materials, and selling spices and goods they'd never seen before. And when he was finished Bard spoke about his plans in Mercia, how he'd build houses with help of Karl and his sons, plough the earth, grow certain crops. It was late afternoon, the weather was warm and sunny, and most of us became dozy from the gentle rocking of the boat, and as there wasn't much else to do, we lied down to rest.

After a short nap, I watched Olfi's dad, who was called Ljot, carving a piece of light wood.

"It's going to be a little horse, for Olfi," he said as I followed his skilled movements.

"You're very good at it," I said.

"Have ye seen the carvings along the side of the ship?" he asked.

"Not yet," I answered.

"Take a look!"

I leaned over the boat ridge and looked up and down the boat. At the end of the boat the edge went upwards, forming a bow, like the tail of an animal. All along the side-wall there was about a 20–30cm wide stripe carved with a pattern containing swirls and dragon heads bitting dragon tails. The front of the boat ended in another bow, larger than the one in the back, and contained an animal head, covered with the swirling patterns. The animal head might have been a dragon or a lizard.

"Do ye know who did these carvings?" Ljot asked.

"Was that you?" I asked.

"Oh, nay!" he said smiling. "This boat was made along time ago—I remember, as a child watching it being made. Most of the carvings ye see were done by me Granddad." And while he said so, he made a movement with his head towards Ragnar.

"Ragnar is your Granddad?" I asked.

"Yes, the father of me father," he answered. "Ragnar has survived his own son. Me father died in a fight, ye see." he added.

"Was that long ago?"

"Some ten sommers," he answered with a quiet sigh.

Ljot was slim and strong, similar to Ragnar, only taller, and his hair was fair blond, whereas Ragnar was grey. Ljot's long hair was tied to the back in a pony tail, his beard was not so long. There was nothing fancy with his beard or hair. This fitted to his character; he was rather quiet and remained in the background.

To keep the conversation going I asked: "Is that your wife?" and I looked over to the young mother who was showing Rohanna how to use a spindle. The baby was asleep in its basket.

"Yes," he said. "She's Astrid."

Astrid too was slim. Her long blond hair was loosely tied to the back framing a narrow tired-looking face. Yet, I had seen her rowing before, and it seemed she had the strength of an ox. Her fingers handled the spindle nimbly and the wool glided down twisting rapidly.

"And what's the name of the baby?" I asked.

"She's Gunnhild," Ljot answered with a mix of pride and humbleness. "Gunnhild was also the name of her Great-Grandmother."

"She's still very small," I said.

"Yeah, she's only a few weeks old. She was born when the raspberries ripened. But now she will grow up in a foreign land and won't know her own country, where she was born!"

"Do you find it easy to travel with a baby?"

"Oh, she's a lot less trouble, then Olaf," Ljot said grinning. "Olfi's like a young deer trapped on a boat. He's a lively-one and needs constantly to be kept busy!"

The afternoon seemed to drag on. The boat moved on in moderate speed, about the pace of a bike on an even road. There was nothing but water, endless water around us. On the one hand, I admired the infinity of the grey-green coloured sea gently rippling against the sides of the boat, reflecting the afternoon sun. On the other hand, there was something dramatic and even fearsome about the sea. Compared to the sea, our boat was tiny and vulnerable—a nut shell drifting on mighty waters. The sea could change any time, if the calm and peaceful surroundings would change into dangerous waves, whipped up by wind and storm.

"If everything goes well," Ragnar reassured, "We'll reach the coast of the Angles' Isles by tomorrow."

The large sail flapped a little in the draught as Ragnar checked the fastenings. The sail had been mended in a few places, and I asked Ragnar, what material it was made of.

"This beauty is made of flax," he said. "And it has endured a lot! Two generations it's lasted, and may last even more."

The red pattern in the middle of the sail depicted a large bird with wings spread out, flying upwards above swirling waves.

"Don't you usually have sails with red and white strips?" I asked, thinking of a typical Viking ship, the kind I was used to seeing on pictures.

"This ship is a Karve," he answered. "Ships with stripes are the ones that go to war. A Karve doesn't have red and white stripes."

"And what is the difference between a Karve and a war ship?" I asked, hoping I didn't sound ignorant.

"This ship is broader, isn't it. That's 'cause we need space for storing goods and animals. A war ship is narrow, long and swift. Have ye ever seen one at sea?"

I shook my head.

"Cor... a pity! With a war ship you're able to travel high speed and carry a lot of men at once. There's none swifter than our war ships."

The boat we were travelling on was around ten metres long and five metres wide. In the middle of the deck there was a square opening, like a hole, where all the baggage was kept and where we had played Hnefatafl. The six rowing benches on each side of the boat were on top of the deck (each bench was also like a chest with items stored away). We slept between the benches on deck, and this was where we were going to spend the next night too.

Chapter Nine—Sea Monster

That evening, we rowed on for another hour. My back and arm muscles were hurting from the previous rowing session, but I tried not to show it. I needed to be tougher, I told myself.

The setting sun reflected on the water, and each time the oars scooped into the sea and out again, they left behind a rippling trail of glittering orange.

"There's a nice current," Bard called out. "That will make rowing lighter!"

He was right. It became easier to pull the oars back, while the underwater current pushed the boat forward. It would soon be night and I looked forward to ending rowing, spreading out the animal skins and wrapping ourselves in our cloaks. The sun turned dark red as it touched the horizon, until it finally got swallowed by the sea. I watched the sun disappear and rested my arms on my oar, while some rowers stood up to stretch their legs. Then curiously I noticed rippling in the water, even though we had stopped rowing. This motion didn't come from the boat: it began somewhere far behind the boat, deep in the sea, and it grew more intense by the minute.

"Does this mean a storm is coming?" I asked Ragnar, who was examining the movement on the sea's surface with Ljot. But Ragnar didn't answer; he seemed completely absorbed in his observations.

Ljot shook his head, saying, "There is not a cloud in the sky, and no wind…"

Ragnar still remained silent. Then he did something unexpected. He sprang down into the square opening of the deck, pushed some bags aside, bent down and placed his ear close to the wooden floor.

"Shhh," he said, concentrating on a sound coming from underneath. After a minute he got up again and said, "This ain't no upcoming storm—course not. It's something else."

"What is it?" asked Helga.

"Speak up, Ragnar, wise old man!" Bard added.

"Yeah, I may be wise," Ragnar answered, "but something is approaching what's beyond me wisdom!"

"Eh, now tell us what this is all about!" Helga demanded.

Karl, Bjorn, Erik and Ljot gathered around Ragnar as he climbed out of the bagging area.

Only Astrid and Rohanna, with the children, remained sitting in the background.

"Well..." Ragnar began, "I'm not sure if yer prepared for this. I'm not prepared meself. But I know what it could be. I've heard it—the rippling is coming from within the sea..."

"What does this mean? C'mon, Ragnar, we're bursting to know!" Bard said.

"Go down and hear for yerself," Ragnar summoned him. Bard jumped down into the same space, and like Ragnar knelt down, pressing his ear to the plank to listen.

"There's a light beat coming from within the sea..." he said, "and it appears to be intensifying."

"And ye can't imagine what that is?" Ragnar asked. I had never seen him look as serious and alert before. "This is no time for resting!" he announced. "Everyone, back to rowing, as if yer life depended on it! In fact, yer life does depend on it! We have to get away from here as fast as possible!"

We all moved back to the deck and glanced at the sea. The water was now dark, almost black, and the rippling had grown into little waves, while darkness spread across the sky like a thick, heavy curtain covering the last bits of light.

"Might it be…" Helga began to ask, half whispering as she held onto the gunwhale.

"A sea monster!" Ragnar completed her question. "I can't tell which one, but you don't want to encounter it. It would simply mean…"

"Death?" Bard asked, and Ragnar nodded.

"To the oars, everyone!" Bard shouted, "And by 'everyone' I mean everyone, expect for the little ones!"

Next thing, everyone jumped to the rowing benches. Karl sat in front of me, after him Rohanna—who rowed for the first time—and in front of her sat Bjorn. Behind me was Helga, and on the other side were Bard, Astrid, Erik and Ljot, with Ragnar taking over the starboard. The waves were now swelling upwards around the boat as we began rowing with all our might.

"Not too quick strokes," Ragnar shouted, as we tended to do short, fast moves in our haste. "Long strokes, long strokes!"

I had learnt the rhythm of rowing earlier in the day. Deep and slow strokes were more effective for moving fast. But now it was hard to stick to that while something terribly threatening was looming behind us.

The waves grew higher, and the boat began to rock. The strong motion made me feel sick. I tried not to think about it and to focus on rowing, but in vain. My stomach turned and I leaned over the brim to throw up, and that a few times. The waves induced wind, the sail puffed up, and the strings hanging down from the sail flapped wildly. The sail trapped the wind, causing the boat to rock even more.

"Get the sail down!" Ragnar shouted. Bjorn and Karl reacted fast. The waves grew even higher and the boat swayed like mad, from one side to the other. One moment the sea rose high, spraying water into the boat; the next moment it seemed we were heading for the sky. The world seesawed from one side to another, as if unable to decide where it wanted us to be.

The roaring of the waves drowned out our voices, and nothing more was spoken, apart from orders shouted by Bard or Ragnar.

Every new wave sprayed water on us, and it wasn't worth dodging them any more. We kept on rowing while getting soaked.

"Keep going, keep going!" Bard shouted. I was feeling less sick now—there was nothing left in my stomach to throw up. Rowing with all my might made me hot and sweaty and I became short of breath, my heart beating strongly. Every time a new gush of water came down on me, it was like taking a cold shower.

The waves grew even bigger. We couldn't escape them, they were crashing all around us. Someone shouted, "There's too much water on board! Quick!" Ljot was first to let go of his oar. He grabbed a leather bucket and began bailing out the excess water.

"No more rowing!" shouted Ragnar. "We've got to lose this water!" I took hold of a wooden jug which was rolling around, and began scooping water from the deck. Then came another huge wave which swamped us again. We all gathered in the centre of the boat. The two children were asleep, tucked under Astrid's arms.

"There ain't much we can do," Ragnar said. "There's only one thing left to hope for!"

"Which is what?" Helga asked.

"That the beast backs away and the sea calms down again."

"But in the sea monster tale, people get washed away to the end of the world!" Helga exclaimed

"To the end of the world?" I asked.

"They were thrown to the very edge of the world—and from there they'd fall down into the abyss!" she shouted, as another heavy wave sprayed the boat, making it rock violently.

"But the earth is round..." I began explaining, when something stopped me from continuing. Behind the boat, some fifty metres away, something dark appeared on the surface of the sea. It looked like a slippery black hill rising out of the sea with water dripping off, and it grew as it moved closer. The closer it came, the more it rose until one mighty thrust from the sea sent sprays of water in all directions, revealing a terrifying, enormous creature.

Ragnar, crouched at the back rudder, cried out: "Jörmungandr!"

Now there were screams and shouts all around me. A long thick neck jutted out of the water, reaching the sky. The head was like an enormous serpent's head with fiery red eyes focusing on the boat. The beast opened its mouth, as if to draw breath, revealing a set of long sharp teeth. I realised that this was only the upper part of the beast. How big the rest of its body must have been! No wonder this had caused metre-high waves. But the worst was yet to come.

The water that had drained off the monster's body as it emerged from the sea now caused the biggest wave yet—higher than a multi-storey house, and crashing down towards us. Within seconds it would swamp the boat. There was a mighty tug and the boat flew up. I was tossed to the side of the boat, held on to the rim, and stared at what I couldn't believe was possible: we were riding on top of a gigantic wave! Then the wave descended and the boat raced through the air. For seconds, we were out in the air, united with the black sky. The thousands of stars now seemed closer. For a moment, I questioned whether the earth truly was round or whether this was the end of the world and we had been tossed over the edge. The wind blew my hair, my tunic flapped, and everything lying around loose flew to the back. Some things must have gone overboard. But what did that matter now? I craned my neck to see where everyone else was. Rohanna was huddled down in the centre of the boat, next to Astrid who had her arms tightly around her two children. Others were holding onto the mast or the edge of the luggage space.

"Hold on tight!" someone shouted. Then the boat came crashing down. The stars turned into shiny racing dots, with the wind stronger than ever. It would take a few seconds for the boat to smack down on the water and dive under, and the depths of the sea to swallow us up.

Within this fragment of time and space, I was prepared to meet death—we would all meet our death, I was sure. I wondered if the impact of the boat hitting the water would kill me, or if I would die from drowning. Anything seemed better than being devoured alive by that sea monster. I closed my eyes tightly, awaiting the final moment of my life. I awaited the smack, when the boat would hit the water, but it didn't happen. I opened my eyes and discovered that we were flying. The sail was fully blown out, allowing the boat to glide through the sky like an eagle with wings spread out. We were sailing onwards through the air, and the wind was carrying our boat as if it were as light as a kite. Nevertheless, the boat was gradually descending and the surface of the water coming closer. And then came the smack as the boat landed. A huge gush of water washed over the edges into the boat. After a few jerks the boat found its position and rested, as if nothing had happened. We were paralysed, and it took us a while to get over the shock.

"Are we in the Afterlife?" Helga asked, breaking the silence.

"Well, if it is, it looks the same as the place we left…" said Bard, glancing around him.

We were surrounded once again by water, but it was a calm sea.

"Everyone's still here!" Ragnar exclaimed, still clutching the rudder. I counted all the occupants and breathed a sigh of relief. We had all survived.

"How is everyone?" Bard asked, short of breath.

But before anyone answered, we noticed that the depth of water in the boat had reached knee-level. This made the boat much heavier and lower, so that the edges were closer to the water surface. The sea was calm, but the heavy boat swayed from side to side, inviting more water to slop over, risking us losing our balance. If we didn't react fast, the boat would sink.

"Quick, everyone!" Bard shouted, and we all grabbed a pot, a bucket, a cup—whatever was left scattered around the boat—and began bailing water. This was when I realised that we had lost most of our baggage, but also the goat and the hens. They hadn't been able to hold onto anything to stop themselves falling off the boat. There was no sign of them. It seemed we had landed far away from where we'd encountered the beast. All that remained were the chests under the benches and one or two single boxes and bags wedged between the deck and the hull. I found a woollen blanket trapped under a box and laid it out on the floor. It absorbed some of the water, so I dragged it to the edge of the boat and squeezed it out into the sea. I was glad the terrifying sea monster was gone, yet I kept looking back to assure myself that its ugly head wouldn't reappear out of the dark water.

Working with the simple means we had, it took a long time to bail out the excess water. We were soaked to the skin and shivering. Only the children were still dry; Astrid and Ljot had managed to shield them from the worst, and they had even been able to sleep most of the time. Our pelts were soaked, including the cloaks we used for sleeping. There was nothing left to keep us warm and dry through the night. Everyone was exhausted. We didn't speak much after what we'd been through.

Half the night passed by. Feeling uncomfortable and cold, I huddled up on a bench as did everyone else, some leaning back to back to keep each other warm. We longed to catch some sleep to shorten the time until sunrise when the sun would warm us and dry out the things that remained.

My sleep was restless, and each time I woke up, I forced myself back to sleep, trying not to focus on the uncomfortable freezing cold wet clothes.

Then finally the sky began to brighten, heralding the approach of sunrise. My clothes had dried a little in the meantime, thanks to the constant breeze together with my body heat. My back and my legs were stiff from lying on the hard bench, so I got up and stretched my limbs. I watched the tip of the rising sun appear over the water, how it grew on the horizon, first red, then orange and then golden, painting a path of shimmering light across the light blue sea. It reminded me of the famous orchestral piece called 'Sunrise' by the Norwegian composer Grieg. When the sun appeared fully rounded, it was as if I would hear the melody of the flutes above floating above the glorious violins, underlined by the warm, deep sounds of the cellos and double basses. 'Sunrise' was one of my favourite tunes, and watching this sunrise whilst at sea brought the whole experience to life: the violins represented the sky, the low instruments the deep waters of the sea, and the flute was the gentle sunlight caressing the water's surface. I wondered if Grieg had seen the same as I was seeing when he composed his piece of music.

The clear sky and immaculate sunrise promised a warm day and a calm sea.

Chapter Ten—Thirst and Hunger

One by one we awoke, all complaining of stiff legs and backs.

"What a night!" Erik said. "But at least we survived," and we all agreed.

The boat drifted along in the late morning sun. No one had picked up an oar since the events of last night, and Ragnar wasn't directing the boat anywhere. Our clothes were mostly dry, and the deck was clear of water. Helga sorted the items that lay scattered around. She shook her head in dismay as she unwrapped the remaining sacks, all soaked with water, and laid the contents—clothes, blankets and other things—out to dry.

"Njord, the sea god, has had mercy on us," Bard said. "We've even survived the great sea monster Jörmungandr!"

"Now we can tell everyone that we've met the sea monster!" Karl said with a proud smile.

"I wonder if anyone will believe us," Bjorn replied.

Bard waved his hand in a declining manner. "The real question is now: where are we? The way we landed back on the sea after flying through the air was nothing short of a miracle! But where are we now? Are we on the route to the Angles, or have we ended up in Unknown Waters?"

"The sun is above us," Ragnar said, rubbing his beard. "In the afternoon I'll be able to tell if we're heading eastwards. That sea monster has managed to throw us off our track and the ship has been drifting aimlessly for hours while we were asleep. How far is it to the north, or to the south…? Perhaps we are on route to the unknown."

"The unknown," Helga repeated with widening eyes.

"As long as we're still alive," Erik said. He glanced at the sea behind the drifting boat. "I'll never forget that wretched monster. I'm forever glad we escaped its fangs!"

"Our resources are limited," Ragnar said. "If we run out of food and water before we reach land, you know what that means…"

"Where are our food supplies and drinking water?" Bard asked his wife, who had now sorted most of the things that had survived.

"It ain't looking good, it ain't looking good," she answered, picking up some empty eggshells.

"Plenty of eggshell, but no whole eggs left. And the hens are gone too. Same with the goat. The sea gods must have accepted them as sacrifices—instead of us humans." She bent down and picked up a brown object from the deck. "What's this? A skin bottle of water! Oh, and under the bench two handfuls of dried meat and … one, two, three, four … five apples. But that's all we've got, I'm afraid. Yes, that's all the food and fresh water we've got…"

"All our rich provisions overboard—I can't believe it!" Bard said, punching his forehead with his fist.

"Oh, let's not complain. It's what the gods wanted—isn't it?"

"Ha, them gods can take care of themselves. But what about us? Are we to drink salty water after this bottle is empty?"

Ragnar took the skin bottle in his hands and peeped inside. "Gonna get difficult without fresh water supplies," he said.

"There's water all around us, but we can't drink it!" Karl added.

"Unless we find a way to get the salt out," Bjorn said.

"Eh, nonsense. How on earth will we do that?" Bard asked, shaking his head.

"We'd need to boil the water and collect the purified water drops," Ragnar said. "But there's little chance of that. What would we burn? There's nothing left. We won't be able to produce fire until we reach land. Odin knows where and when that will be…!"

We all gathered in the middle of the boat and Helga passed the leather bottle around.

"Each one sip and no more!" she demanded. She cut two apples into twelve thin slices. "There's one each, and Astrid gets two 'cause she's nursing!" she said, handing out each person their ration. After that, everyone got to work. There was still more to tidy up and untangle.

While everyone was busy, Olfi said aloud, "Pafi," turning to Ljot, "I dreamt something strange!"

"Speak up," his dad said, and everyone else was curious to hear too.

"There was a storm in my dream. It was lightening and thundering and everything was messed up on the boat."

"That's how it looks now, doesn't it," Ljot said.

"Well, we 'ave been through a kind of storm," Helga said, winking and swaying her head from left to right, as if she was evaluating the situation.

"But you were fast asleep all the time, weren't you?" Astrid asked, stroking Olfi's blond mop of hair.

"Yeah, I think so. But I ain't finished telling me dream. In this dream, I sat up, 'cause I saw something terrible: a very huge animal. It was looking out of the water, right there, behind the bow of the ship. It had glowing red eyes. It looked straight at me. But I hid under me Modir's arm," he said, looking up to Astrid, "and I carried on sleeping, didn't I, Modir? And the terrible monster went away. When I woke up, I was so glad it had only been a dream!"

Everyone fell silent (apart from baby Gunnhild who whimpered). Bard was looking out to sea while holding the boat rim, and turned around. With a serious expression he said, "What a terrible dream…" and the others looked at one another or at the ground, in embarrassment, not sure whether to say something or not.

The morning passed with the gnawing feeling of hunger and not knowing where we were. Ragnar had found out, meanwhile, that we had gone eastwards, but he didn't know how far north we were. The afternoon sun scorched down on us, yet the air was cool with a constant breeze, and I couldn't make up my mind if I was feeling too cold or too warm. My stomach grumbled. Images of rich meals kept popping up in my head, especially when I tried to suppress them. I almost smelt the delicious smell of steaming potatoes, fried egg, sausages, green peas, or then a lamb roast sizzling over the fire in the Anglo-Saxon village hall. Hunger banged at my inner door, like an unwelcome guest. But our next meal consisted of only another sip of water, a slice of dried deer meat and a piece of apple. The same was planned for supper, and then our rations would be finished.

Karl and Erik tried catching fish with a small piece of bread hanging on a leather belt for a bait and a makeshift hook made of a spare nail. They tried for an hour each without success. But then again, I wasn't sure if raw fish was edible.

The hours seemed to pass more slowly than usual. Ragnar advised us now and then to row, while keeping to the east. Yet he wasn't sure whether we were rowing for our good or for the worst. Rowing used up more of our energy, which without nutrition was barely existent.

I let one arm hang over the boat's side, weak from the involuntary fast. I glanced into the water, wondering if I could spot seaweed in our need for food, but the water was too deep for plants to reach near the surface. How long was this lack of food going to last, I asked myself. What if it went on for days? It terrified me to imagine how the situation would deteriorate without food or fresh water.

There were two children on board, and a young mother—and how would Rohanna cope, and all the others?

"We must look out for signs of land, it's our only hope," Ragnar said. "Land will save us from dying of hunger—at least we could possibly hunt a wild animal and find edible plants…"

"Not a sign of land anywhere," Helga said, emphasising what everyone else could see for themselves. Ljot looked east, but a rising mist covered everything to the horizon.

We hardly talked that afternoon. I played a game of Hnefatafl with Karl, but before the second round ended, he went to lie down. An empty stomach made it difficult to concentrate on a game. I too lay down on the bare deck planks and stared up at the sky, thinking about how to get out of this, but there seemed to be no solution. I closed my eyes, and when I licked my dry lips, all I got was the taste of salt sticking to my face. Suffering from hunger at sea was worse than being lost in a forest, where you might come across a berry bush, some edible mushrooms or roots, or an animal to hunt. You could make a fire, even without matches, if you tried hard enough. But out in the open sea there was nowhere to go, nothing to discover; there was just water and water all around—water you couldn't drink. I began to hate the smell of the sea, mixed with fish and algae. The immense stretch of blue water under the cavernous sky looked beautiful, but it was a deadly beauty. At sea you might feel free, but this was now a dangerous freedom. I tried to block all worries out. The boat rocked gently as the water splish-splashed against the outer planks, the mast creaked with each breeze, and the sail flapped intermittently. This would be the kind of relaxation you'd enjoy on a holiday, but instead we were on a deadly journey somewhere out on the Unknown Waters.

The sun was nearing the horizon, and as it sank, our hopes of discovering land sank too. The mist had formed into clouds—great grey clouds rolling towards us.

"Take down the sail!" Ragnar ordered. "There will be rain," he said, observing the grey clouds. And soon enough, the first raindrops started drumming down. Erik, Bjorn, Bard and Karl undid the sail and stretched it from one side of the boat to the other, creating a roof. Before long a shower of rain was pouring down on the makeshift roof. Some of the rain trickled in from the sides and developed puddles on the deck. The temperature sank fast, and soon we were shivering once again. The only consolation was the sail above our heads that kept off most of the heavy rain.

Chapter Eleven—Kraken

In the two days that had passed since we had set out on this voyage, Rohanna and I had barely had an opportunity to talk privately. Now we were sitting side by side trying to keep warm under the sail, and while the others were talking with each other to distract themselves from their misery, Rohanna and I exchanged a few words about what had been in the back of our minds all this time.

"I keep asking myself what century we are in now," Rohanna whispered.

"It's got to be the time of the Vikings," I answered. "But I can't tell which period. If I had paid more attention at the museum, I might've known. Everything was explained in detail... When did the Norse emigrate to England—was it just at the beginning of the Viking era or throughout the whole period?"

"I'm also wondering how much time has passed since we left Mercia... I mean, we *are* young again, we can't be much older than when we left Mercia, so perhaps just a couple of years have gone by?" she asked with hope in her voice.

"If this is the age of the Vikings, it could be anything between one and 300 years that have passed!"

"What makes you come up with that number?"

"Think of it ... Viking raids on Britain began at the end of the eighth century. Remember Durwyn's dad? He had already fought against the Vikings when we were there. The Viking invasions then ended around the first millennium—so, around 1000 something. We've got to be somewhere within those 300 years."

Rohanna shuddered. "We'll find out as soon as we reach Hamberton. The monks will be able to tell the year."

She didn't mention the village where Durwyn came from, but I knew she was mostly concerned about him. If any time had passed, I hoped it was only a few years. But what if decades or even centuries had gone by? This time it was I who shuddered, and not just from cold and hunger. The idea of returning to Mercia and finding out that all our friends had died long ago would be hard to take.

As we were all trapped under the roof with nothing to do and with our energy diminishing, one after the other began telling a tale to pass the time and make our situation more bearable. It definitely helped to distract our minds from thinking about food or rather the lack of it. They must have told each other these tales before, because from the comments made in between, it sounded as if each listener already knew the story. Yet there was something comforting about listening to another person narrating, and so they seemed pleased to listen to it all over again. When Ljot came to the end of his tale (before him, Helga, Bard and Ragnar had been narrating), Bard turned to me and asked: "What about ye? Do ye 'ave a tale? You must 'ave something in store that we ain't heard yet!" I wanted to answer: "No, not really," because, what could I tell them? I had spent most of my life living pleasantly and comfortably in modern Britain.

"Ye must know some saga from the land of the Angles!" he pushed.

I shrugged my shoulders. I wasn't good at telling stories. Maybe Rohanna could make one up? I glanced over at her, but she raised her eyebrows and pouted her lips as if to say: "No, not me … you go ahead!"

"Come on," I signalled with my eyes. "You know I'm not good at this…" But Rohanna just blinked confidently —she had made up her mind.

And then I *did* remember. Of course I knew a tale or a saga. It was the one with Ethón. The one I had been through myself!

"Well, there is a Mercian story about a dragon emerging from its lair every seven years…" I began, but hesitated. Was I ready to explain to our new friends that Rohanna and I didn't originate from this age and this world? She and I were people from a modern world—but could they ever understand that? I decided to tell the story in the third person, as if it was someone else and not me who had been through it all. More slowly than usual (my exhaustion didn't allow me to talk energetically) I spoke of a young boy who had experienced all the adventures I had been through, without mentioning that the boy was me.

I began with the prophecy, the way I had heard it from the storyteller many years ago in the village hall. I wasn't as good at narrating as the storyteller had been, but when it came to the parts which involved myself (my call to slay the dragon, the quest I went on, wise Halig, the monks, evil Wicka, the talking trees, the fairies and dwarfs)—everything came alive, as if it had happened yesterday. I felt again the fear when I was alone in the cell, haunted by the evil blue spirit, or when lost in the forest. I remembered how Wicka had drugged me and didn't want to let me go, and the terrifying beast in the dark, damp, hot lair, as well as the triumph over its death before the icy blue spirit reappeared; then the battle with the dwarfs and our race back to Durwyn's home with the healing potion to save his sister. My listeners remained silent all along. Even when I stopped, they were still quiet for a while.

Bard broke the silence when he said, "A strange place that Mercia must be! But also a true hero that young dragon slayer!" and the others nodded. They were now too exhausted to make further comments. Nobody asked how I knew this tale; it seemed normal for them to hear all sorts of stories and sagas. My story was just another tale for their repertoire, and they'd keep it alive by passing it on among their people.

After I had finished my tale, my desire to be back in Mercia grew stronger. I was looking forward more than ever to getting back. I felt the kind of prickling excitement you get when you're going to meet old friends or places you haven't seen for a long time. I wanted to jump up and see if there was land in sight. But I was too weak, just like everyone else. Rohanna sat with her arms wrapped round her knees, her face buried in her arms. Perhaps she was hiding tears—tears of nostalgia, anticipation and hope?

Meanwhile it had turned dark. Some of the travellers wrapped themselves in blankets, which had dried during the day, and soon fell asleep.

I wrapped my arms around my legs, rested my head on my knees and slipped into a slumber. I dreamt of the hotel room in Norway, and then my own bedroom back in England. In my dream I woke up and told someone I had dreamt of being on a boat. I regretted waking up, even though I was safe and comfortable. Then towards the end of this confusing dream, I realised that I was neither in the hotel room, nor in my bedroom. I opened my eyes and despite the cold, hunger and uncertainty of where we were going, I was strangely glad to find myself on the boat. The sky had cleared and above me a million stars twinkled, reassuring me that this world was real, before I fell asleep once more.

"What's that rip-rapping?" Bard asked, tugging me out of my sleep.

"Doesn't sound like rain," Ragnar said. He sat up, alert.

The rip-rapping came from the left side of the sail. It sounded like slobbery scratches. It couldn't have been rain, because rain is continuous. The rapping lasted for a few seconds, paused, then carried on.

"We have to take a look," Bard said. "I'll go and lift the sail!" It was still stretched out to protect us from rain and wind.

"Caution!" Ragnar warned. He stood up and held Bard back by the arm. "What if it's a living creature? Only lift a tiny bit of the sail, just enough to get a glimpse. Don't reveal a lot—whatever it is, we don't wanna provoke it!"

Bard didn't need to lift the sail, because at the moment the tip of a thick, slippery tentacle appeared. I wondered if an octopus had got caught up in our boat, but soon dismissed that idea. The tentacle flopped into the space where we were gathered. It was black and green and as thick as the thickest snake I had ever seen, and it flopped up and down. The stench of rotting fish spread around.

"Back, back," Ragnar shouted to the women. And then, "Bard, boys! Pull out yer knives! This must be Kraken, the Enormous Octopus! There's no surviving its attack unless we manage to harm all its arms. If not, we'll get dragged down into the sea!"

The men were carrying daggers in their belts, and in no time they clutched them in their hands, ready to attack. Every dagger was now necessary. As one tentacle came up from one side of the boat, another appeared on the other side. Then all of a sudden there were tentacles on every side!

"Move to the middle!" Ragnar shouted to those who weren't armed. The boat rocked wildly—not because of the people moving around, but from the weight of the tentacles. There were about six or seven of them now, and they clearly belonged to a ginormous creature. They were all over the boat. Then the sail ripped off to expose the sight of an ugly beast with enormous tentacles, and we realised that only the tips of its many limbs had reached the boat.

Ljot began slashing his knife at a tentacle that was threatening Astrid, desperately shielding the children. And then all I saw was Bard, Ragnar, Karl and the two brothers jumping around, slashing and stabbing the tentacles that by now had caused the boat to rock so hard that it was bound to capsize at any moment. The creature seemed determined to strangle the boat, the people and all. The men had to react quickly. I regretted not having a knife or sword on me. Helplessly, I watched the fight between men and tentacles. Apart from the slobbery rip-rapping, the creature made no sound. The blows of the weapons made it angry and it rebelled and attacked with even more determination.

"Take yer swords, for Odin's sake!" Bard shouted. "The daggers ain't enough!" The terribly thick tentacles were only getting lightly wounded. The men hastily dug for their swords in the chests, and the fight against the Kraken became fiercer. Deep wounds appeared on several of the monster's arms. The boat rose up one more time, then Kraken pulled back its wounded arms and vanished into the dark depths. It wasn't seen again.

Water had filled the boat once more. But if we were all exhausted before Kraken's attack, now we were even more fatigued. And what was worse, the sail was ripped in several places. With the last of our strength, but lacking motivation, everyone started bailing again. But our movements were slow and some were near giving up.

The rain had stopped. The stench of rotting fish and sea tang hung still in the air, and black slime stuck on the foredeck. It made me feel sick, but my stomach was empty with nothing left to throw up.

"When am I going to get a sword too?" Olfi suddenly asked, still sitting close to Astrid. He hadn't been asleep this time.

Ljot paused in shovelling water, realising that his young son had not been spared the sight of Kraken. "You're going to have to grow a bit first, and then, son!" he answered.

Karl, the two brothers and Astrid began repairing the sail with strong twine. It didn't take long before the sail was pulled up again. The wind propelled us away from where

Kraken had attacked. I didn't know if this was leading us in the right direction, but I didn't care any more. Nobody seemed to care any more. Slumped on benches and the deck, all we wanted was to get away and forget what we had seen; enough of sea monsters, enough of the terror. We were cold, weak and hungry, and even if there had been some survival energy left in us during the encounter with Kraken, it was certainly used up now. If anything else happened, all would be over. Nobody would have the energy to fight. But even without anything happening, our end was bound to come. Deprived of nutrition and drinking water, our time was limited. Starvation and dehydration knocked impatiently on our door, eager to take our diminishing lives away … unless a miracle happened and land came in sight. I looked around, but there was nothing to be seen apart from mist rising from the sea.

Chapter Twelve—Pictland

After some time, Ragnar ordered us to take the sail down and let the boat drift. We wrapped ourselves in whatever woollen coats and blankets were left and gave ourselves up to sleep—the only effective distraction from our calamity. I slept until after sunrise. When I awoke the mist was still present, but I could see about two hundred metres around us.

"This morning, no breakfast. Either the gods wish us well and will bring us to land, or they are taking revenge on us and we will find death in the Endless Water..." Helga spoke hoarsely and tightened the blanket around her as she sat on a bench.

"It had better be soon," Bard mumbled, close to her. His voice was quieter than usual.

"The mist might mean we're not far from land," Ragnar added.

"Whatever land that may be?" Bard asked.

"That doesn't matter now, does it? All we need is wild animals for meat, and some rest!"

"Them gods!" Helga carried on in a bitter tone. "I wonder if they care at all!"

"Don't make it worse by enraging them!" Bard warned.

"It couldn't get any worse, after what we've been through ... could it?" Helga croaked, shaking her head and looking out to sea.

Whether it was their pagan Viking gods or our Christian God who might intervene, something would have to happen soon if we were destined to survive. Rohanna sat on a bench by the edge, resting her head on her arms, leaning on the railing. She might have been praying and reflecting on her life ending. What else was there left to do? Death seemed close. Like her, I didn't talk. Each movement, each spoken sentence used up energy which we were unable to replace, due to lack of food. All that was left to do was to stare at the undrinkable water.

The sun burned down from its zenith, and the travellers were all silent. Olfi had long stopped running excitedly from one place to another. He wasn't asking questions any more. His head rested on his mother's knees. Astrid nursed the baby, but it was unsettled and didn't seemed to be getting enough milk.

In my mind, I prepared myself for perishing from thirst and starvation. How long would it take? Was it going to be painful? Would some of us soon begin hallucinating? A sudden movement struck the corner of my eye. Erik sat up and pointed to the sky, whispering croakily, "A bird! It's a seagull!"

"What's the big deal?" I thought to myself, unimpressed. But all the others seemed uplifted from the sight of the bird. Did they want to shoot it for dinner? But how? I hadn't seen any bow and arrow on board, so how would they get hold of the bird? Hit it with a heavy object?

It wasn't the only seagull: soon five or six of them were circling above the sail.

Bard raised both arms, as if worshipping the sky. "Oh, what joy! What good news you bring!" and the others joined in with claps and smiles.

I began to wonder if this might be the first signs of madness, but then I realised it could be our next meal:

"How are you going to catch them? And how are you going to cook them?"

"Eh, don't ye understand?" Erik croaked excitedly. "Don't ye get what this means? It means land, land, *land!*"

Ragnar crawled back to the rudder and steered the boat in a new direction. He appeared to know exactly what he was doing. "Sail down, and get rowing!" he ordered. "After the seagulls we go!"

I dragged myself to my oar and rested both hands on the wood, holding onto it to support my weakened body. I wondered how to gather enough strength for the physical work required. If I was to survive, I had to give everything that was left. In slow motion I pulled the oar back, let it dip in the water and tugged it out again. We were all rowing more slowly than usual, but at least we were moving forward filled with hope.

More seagulls gathered around our boat. Their *keow, keow, keow* cries sounded like music to our ears. If this meant land, then these seagulls were angels, messengers of hope. And sure enough, the mist diminished, revealing a grey, dull sky. But beneath it, in the distance, we saw masses of rock! With each oar stroke plunging in and out of the water, the rocks came closer and closer.

Ragnar steered the boat with great care along the coast. High, steep rocks towered over the water, making it impossible to land. The waves were constantly drawing us towards the cliffs, but we had to keep the boat from hitting them. Some rocks projected out of the water like sharp miniature mountains. Waves smacked against the dark, grey masses of the cliffs, and it took more strength and concentration to keep the boat from being pushed into the rocks than sailing on the open sea. We moved past the rocks until the coast levelled off in a sandy strip, suitable for landing. The beach was a narrow patch of sand lying between the rocky masses, and beyond the rocks stretched a green treeless landscape. Never in my life was I happier to see land again!

Bard, Erik, Bjorn and Karl got off the boat and into the water, nearly submerged to their hips. They helped land the boat on the beach by pushing and tugging on all sides. We all got out, stepped into the cold water and helped drag the boat onto the dry sand. It was hard work, especially with no strength left. With great effort, and each of us close to collapsing, we pushed the boat far enough onto the sand that it could not get washed back into the sea.

"Heave ho!" the men croaked as they pushed and tugged the heavy boat inch by inch further up the dry sand. We were so focused on our hard work that we didn't notice the group of men standing on a raised green ledge above the beach, watching us from above.

"That will do!" Bard called out when the boat was a few yards away from the water. Just as we paused, someone nudged Bard and nodded toward the group of around nine men, as still as statues, each with a spear in his hand.

"We are here in peace, remember," Bard whispered. But were *they?* With their weapons ready at hand, what were we to expect?

"Give them a sign of peace. Then we must walk up to them and greet them," Ragnar said. "That way we'll prove that we ain't here to attack." Acting as a kind of group leader, Bard saluted with his hand up in the air and bowed deeply, clearly enough for them to recognise from their watching point.

We huddled together and stepped cautiously across the sand until our feet touched grass. We couldn't have looked much like a threat, rather like a bunch of derelicts, barely able to uphold ourselves. It was strange to be on land again. The ground seemed to carry on rocking, as was constantly the case at sea. To reach the spot where the group of men stood, we had to climb over some boulders. But once we reached the grassy platform, an endless green landscape dotted with clusters of long coarse grass, speckled with white flowers and bushes of heather stretched far beyond. The sky was grey and the air was fresh. The men were dressed like warriors, and didn't move. For a moment I even wondered if they were real.

They didn't utter a sound, but as we approached them, I could see that their eyes followed us.

"We come in peace!" Bard repeated, his voice sounding scratchy from not drinking. We fellow voyagers nodded in agreement; yet still no reaction from the group of warriors.

One of them carried a longer shield than the others, and appeared to be the leader. His hair was dark and long, mingled with single grey hairs. The men didn't react to what Bard said. Instead they seemed to grip their spears more tightly.

Then Bard leant over to me and hissed, "Approach him in your language and say who we are!"

"Me?" I asked, surprised.

"Go ahead, boy, let's not make 'em more suspicious. We ain't fit for a fight. Look how whacked we are!"

"But what if they don't talk my language?" I protested. After drifting for days at sea, this could be any island or country somewhere in the north (it was rather chilly here). Had we reached the British Isles, or had we drifted further away? Perhaps we had reached a country like Iceland or Greenland, or some unknown island of the North Sea?

"Just give it a try, man!" he said.

Then I remembered how Rohanna and I were able to speak the language of the Norse, even though we had never learnt it. Perhaps it would work this time too.

My knees were shaky as I approached the group of warriors. My body failed to respond, partly from not having eaten properly for two days, and partly because I was standing unarmed in front of nine men carrying weapons and observing me. They were strongly built, tall men with long, dark hair, which the sea wind was blowing dramatically back, presenting unmoved, bearded faces and clever dark beady eyes. Apart from the leader, who may have been in his forties, they were mostly young, around

25 years old, and they looked as if they'd done a lot of physical work, warfare training or both—they were like a repetition of the rocks standing tall and firm against the sea and the wind.

"Hello," I called up to the leader. A hint of curiosity and expectation shone up in his eyes—but no fear. My humble and unarmed appearance was in contrast to their pose of power and strength. I was curious to know where we were and what people they represented.

"We are searching for Mercia, the land of the Angles!" I began. "What is this land here called?"

"Pictland!" the leader announced in a low voice. He didn't change his position, although he may have loosened his grip on the spear.

"Pictland?" I repeated—and my mind started to rotate: *Pictland, Pictland* ... I must have heard this name before … but where was Pictland and what time in history was this? Then suddenly I remembered—yes, Pictland! Wasn't that a lost kingdom of the north? If that was the case, then this would be what we would call in modern language Scotland! Scotland was up north, a long way from Mercia, but at least we had made it to the British Isles. I needn't worry any more about having landed in some unknown, foreign country.

"Are you the Pict people?" I asked, ignited with excitement. I vaguely remembered learning about this mysterious people from images and history books, but hardly knew anything about them.

The chieftain nodded his head, his dark brown eyes gazing steadily at me. "Yes, we're the Picts. Where are you from? And what do you seek?" I noted the rolling Rs in his accent. "As Picts, we do not let ourselves be invaded. We have fought the Romans and the Anglo-Saxons and we will fight against any intruder, no matter how strong or weak they are!" The other men agreed without words; straightening their upright posture and pushing out their chests, they looked even more proud and noble than before.

How was I to answer the chieftain's question? Rohanna and I weren't Vikings. We came from England (or Mercia)—but both countries could sound like a threat to them.

"We have travelled from far," I began, and introduced my fellow travellers with an open-handed gesture. "Most of us are from Norway." The chieftain raised his eyebrows without responding.

"Norway is far across the sea to the east," I said, pointing back to the sea. "Our friends are Vikings, but my sister and I are English, I mean we are from Mercia." Our group of travellers gathered closer around me. It had become apparent to them that I was able to converse with the strangers.

"Tell them we are here for peaceful reasons!" Bard mumbled to me without taking his eyes off the group of warriors, as if afraid they might attack after all.

"Why don't you mention it yourself?" I asked him.

"How—if I can't speak the language you both are talking?"

Then I realised that, once again, I was capable of understanding a language that otherwise would be foreign to me.

"These Vikings are peaceful and do not want to hurt anyone," I said, directing my attention to the Pict chieftain again. "They are seeking new land to live in. But not here in Pictland; in Mercia, further south, where the Anglo-Saxons live." He nodded thoughtfully and mumbled something to the others, but too quiet for me to hear.

The next thing I thought was necessary was to make sure we had something to eat—and soon. I was still able to stand and talk, but what about the women and the children? I didn't want their health to be at risk for any longer. This was an emergency and so I dared to ask: "Please, could you help us by letting us know where to get food?"

Rohanna joined in and said, "There are two little children in our group, and we are all very hungry!" She too was able to speak this foreign language! But there was no time to ponder on it. I noticed she was dizzy and could hardly stand as she grasped my arm.

"We have lost all our food provisions at sea," I continued. "The waters were rough and we were lost at sea for several days." I also translated to Bard and the others that I was now asking for help.

"Tell him we 'ave things to trade!" Bard added.

"Yes, there's plenty of amber. We can pay for food and lodging! But we need urgent help," Helga said.

I asked the chieftain if he was interested in trading. But he shook his head.

"We do not take foreign ware," he said with his rolling Rs.

The chieftain turned to his men and they had a brief discussion. Then he beckoned us to follow.

A sigh of relief ran through our group. I also sensed relief coming from the chieftain and his men too. Observing our boat from afar, they had probably expected us to be fierce warriors and raiders; but in the end it turned out that we were a bunch of pitiful hungry people.

Everyone grabbed a handful of possessions from the boat, and we took up the march behind the Picts. We walked down a slope towards an endless meadow that went so far that it touched the sky on the horizon. Nearby I spotted two groups of round houses forming small settlements. We arrived at the first group of round huts where two tall rectangular stones stood in the grass, marking the entrance of the settlement. The stones enclosed the shape of a wide cross that was filled with decorative circles and repeating swirls.

Two dozen round houses were set out in a wide circle, with vegetable beds grouped behind each and in the centre a large fireplace. The round houses were each about 10 metres in diameter with thatched roofs made from a thick layer of straw. The walls were chalky white and without windows, the wooden doors decorated with the same circles and swirls as seen on the tall stones at the village entrance. Behind the houses, oat fields swayed in the wind, in the meadows nearby there grazed sheep and cows, undisturbed by the newcomers.

The chieftain and the other men spoke to the women from the houses, and soon they were busy preparing food. Delicious smells of roasted meat wafted over from a spit in the fireplace, reawakening my appetite which had been starved by these days of involuntary fasting. Half an hour later we gathered around the fireplace, each with a wooden bowl on our lap. The women served a stew with big chunks of carrots, onions and meat. The stew warmed my hands through the bowl, and each spoonful of steaming stew warmed my entire body. I ate more slowly than usual, each spoonful of this treat a silent act of thanksgiving. After the stew we were served roasted lamb from the spit, white cheese and scrambled eggs and warm milk to drink. It took a while for the nutrition to revive our bodies, but after the meal we regained our strength.

The chieftain came over to Bard and me to talk.

"My name is Drest," he introduced himself, "son of Gest, the Pictish tribe leader of the Caledoni."

"Bard, my name is Bard. A son of the Norse tribe."

"Where do you intend to go?" Drest asked as I translated for both.

"Tell him we hope to go down south where the weather is mild and the grass is green and lush: the land of the Angles, that place where ye and yer sister will lead us."

Drest nodded and repeated what he had said earlier: "We have successfully kept the Angles and Saxons away from our land, as with the Romans before. We are a people that do not want to be ruled by others."

Bard listened to my translation, his eyes drifting into the distance, disclosing a hint of pain and weariness. "We have lost a lot at sea," he said warily. "I'm sure it wouldn't 'ave happened if the gods didn't wanna punish us. They sent us twice terrible sea monsters to deal with! Yet we're lucky we got away with our lives... Yes, indeed. Everyone of us 'ave gone through the horrible torments, but we each survived, 'aven't we, and I don't know which of the gods I should thank and blame for what we've been through." He shifted his legs, and his expression became more businesslike. "If you wish, we 'ave amber left and some weaponry to exchange for yer generosity."

Drest ignored his offer, but picked up on what Bard had said before: "We don't believe in several gods. We believe that there is only one true God."

"You have only one god?" Bard asked, astonished.

"Yes, it's the One who created everything!" Drest said, pointing up to the sky. "The heavens and earth. It is the One True and Holy God. Nothing else is greater than Him."

Bard produced a half-smile. "Well, I guess that makes matters easier. At least you can tell who's responsible for everything..."

In the meantime, Helga had spread out some of the golden-sandy amber stones and a couple of decorated daggers on a blanket. Some of the villagers looked over our shoulders at the treasures, finding it hard to hide their curiosity. But the chieftain shook his head and waved his hand in defence. "No, no. We don't need any payment whatsoever. As Christians it is our honour and glory to give hospitality to honourable people. You have suffered a lot. You shall rest and regain your strength. Ask for anything you need, and we will help where we can."

After a pause he asked, "Is the young red-haired girl the only unmarried woman you have with you?"

There were only three, and one could tell that Astrid and Helga were married, as they were busy with their husbands and children, and they also carried veils that covered most of their hair. Helga was middle-aged, and one would naturally expect her to be married with children;

Astrid had small children, almost constantly around her. But the third young girl was Rohanna, and now his attention focused on her.

"Astrid is married to Ljot, and Helga to Bard," I explained, pointing to them and their children. "Erik and Bjorn are the children of Helga and Bard; and Ljot and Astrid's children are Olaf and the baby girl."

"And this young girl—is she *your* bride-to-be?" he asked with a nod towards Rohanna.

"Oh, no. She's my sister," I said, wondering what would come next.

"So, she's unmarried and not given away?"

"Yes, still unmarried," I said truthfully.

"We have quite a few good young men," the chieftain continued and beckoned Rohanna closer. She understood what was going on and put up a polite smile, which I knew did not mean she was in for the deal.

I hesitated with an answer, but since the chieftain was talking over her to me, I said: "She is already promised to someone in our land, and we are on our journey back there, where he lives."

"Are you sure?" he asked, now directing his question to Rohanna. "Our men are strong and healthy. Here in Pictland, as a married woman, you could own a large piece of land. Our women are strong too. We live in a land of freedom. You should consider taking one of our unwed men. They are good Christians and they're good-looking too!" he added with a proud smile. He called over to a group of young people, and before Rohanna could fend off his suggestion, three young men stood in front of us. "This is Gartnait, Eoganan and Tristram," he said, presenting the well-built, tall men. Two of them might have belonged to the group of warriors who we had first met on our arrival. "Three good Christian men, and good fighters!" he said, looking for approval from the three men. They didn't stir much apart from showing a faint smile. Despite their strong appearance, they seemed oddly shy in Rohanna's presence. "So, what do you think?" Once again the chieftain directed his talk towards me, awaiting an answer to the offer. I gave Rohanna a side-look to see what her opinion was. She lowered her eyes and shook her head discreetly, yet clearly enough for me to grasp her meaning.

"That's very kind—your offer is greatly appreciated," I played their game. "But she must first see how things stand with the man who is waiting for her."

"Well, you don't have to decide right away," the Pict said. "But if you go back to your land and it turns out the one you're waiting for is not available any more, you can come back to us Picts! We are a welcoming nation, you see," he said proudly. "We welcome women from other tribes, as it's good for the growth of our people!" and with that he patted the backs of the young warriors, indicating they could go back to where they'd been.

Then there was music and dance for the evening. The music came from flat drums beaten by single men and women, with two or three flutes accompanying them on the high notes. We sat in a circle, some of the women and men singing and clapping. I could see how the three young men Drest had introduced earlier were trying to approach Rohanna. She would even chat with one or the other, but rather out of respect, and not wanting to appear rude by ignoring them. After all, we were guests, and much obliged for the help and hospitality of these people.

The dance was a strange kind of dance which I had never seen before. The women would bow a little then lift their long dress only above their ankle and do a little jump, landing on the front part of the feet. There were women in one line and men in a line opposite, approaching each other and parting again. The men would stomp towards the women, while the women skip-hopped. Our group got dragged into the beating rhythm of the dance, and although I never considered myself a dancer, it was quite easy to follow. And as you didn't have to hold or touch anyone, I didn't stumble over anyone's feet. All the tiredness and weariness I had felt before were now blown away with the flying tune of the flutes, the enchanting drum beat and the fireside sparks, shooting up from the fireplace to the darkening sky.

When it was already dark, Drest brought us to a round hut and said, "This is for the overnight stay of our honoured guests." The straw roof of the round hut reached far down, almost touching the ground. There were no windows, only a high, broad wooden door with shorter straw above.

"Oh, we can set up a tent," Bard said. "We still have the sail and some poles left over."

"No, no," the chieftain insisted. "This is better and warmer. We have a cold strong wind here, up north. Even in summer you can feel its harshness at times. Inside you are better protected than under a sail. There's also a hearth inside." He lifted the bolt and pushed open the heavy wooden door and beckoned us to enter. It smelt damp inside. Almost complete darkness enwrapped us until our eyes became accustomed to the dim light. There was the welcome sight of raised beds along the walls, covered with straw and animal skins. "Women sleep left and men right," he explained, pointing along the prepared beds. "I will send my wife to kindle the fire for the night!"

"That's great," Bard said with relief in his voice, looking around. We hadn't seen such "luxury" for days. Everyone else seemed to breathe out too. After days of rough sleeping at sea, the prospect of a comfortable and peaceful resting place, without unknown dangers lurking in the waters, was most pleasing. "I think we'll be able to set off tomorrow after our recovery. We'll need to set sail again, as long as the weather is on our side."

Drest explained how we should first follow the coast westwards: we'd pass the kingdom of Dal Riada on the west coast, and if we were lucky would be welcomed to stay on land; then we'd travel on down south until we reached the land of Cymry. After that we would enter Mercia, the land of the Angles.

"How long will this journey take?" Bard asked Drest.

"It may be a few days, if all goes well," the chieftain answered. "We will help you with food provisions and furs and anything else you need," he added.

Their generosity was almost overwhelming, and it was hard to imagine what we would have done if we'd never met them.

Next morning, after a good night's rest and waking with the comforting knowledge that we were on safe land, surrounded by helpful people, and strengthened in mind and body, we were again fit for journeying on.

The Picts carried sacks of food, pelts, blankets and drinking water to our boat, which we heaved-hoed back to the water. The tide was high and it was good weather for taking off—a light wind, a fair sky and no storm in sight. Half the village came down to see us off. And even though we had only met the day before, it felt like we were good friends having to part from each other. Even though the men were tough on the outside, I detected a touch of sadness in their eyes. When our group was ready for sailing away, the women and children waved and called farewell, and Drest gave us his blessing. I felt a sting pierce my heart, for would we ever meet again? Besides their friendship and honour, these Picts had provided us with all the material and nutrition we needed. We'd given them nothing in return—unless it was our respect, and we would treasure them forever in our hearts.

Bard stretched out his hand to Drest. "Tell me whatever I can do for ye," he asked.

The chieftain replied, "Pray for my soul, my wife, my family, my people. Pray to my Lord in heaven—He is also the Lord of the Norse…"

Bard sighed. "Someone has to tell me more about yer strange, unique God. But rest assured, if that's all yer asking for … ye have me promise!"

And with that we set off. A couple of Picts helped push the boat down the beach until it floated freely. We waved back to the group of people standing on the beach watching us leave. As we distanced ourselves from the coast, our Pict friends got smaller and smaller until they became unrecognisable on the brown stripe of sandy beach, with the grey cliffs and the green land behind it.

Ragnar was at the rudder, steering us westwards. In the afternoon the wind stirred. The sail was up and we let the boat sail onwards, driven by the wind. The coast remained constantly to our left, some 300 metres away, visible as a grey strip in the distance. We enjoyed a meal of fresh cheese and oatmeal bread, and then played games and travelled on for many hours until the sun neared the horizon, ready to end the day.

Chapter Thirteen—Cymry

The next night we spent on the boat. It was cool, but we were dressed in dry clothes and wrapped in woollen blankets with furry pelts to lie on, and we were well fed too. We had already passed the point in the west after which our direction was to turn south. Strengthened from our last night's indoor rest and the rich food and fresh water, we decided to carry on with the journey through the night. And so the boat drifted southwards as we slept.

Next morning the weather was warmer, as we had left the north wind behind us. The landscape changed from cliffs to long beaches. Perhaps there would be ports and towns too. But we kept away from the coast, to stay clear of local populations.

"In such busy places, we'd get chased away, attacked, captured, whatever..." Ragnar observed. "People expect us to be raiders—a threat to them!"

And so we travelled on. Towards the end of the next day, Bard presumed that we were sailing along the Cymry kingdom, bordering with Mercia. There were cliffs again on our left (occasionally interrupted by small beaches) and small, rocky islands scattered near the coast. Further south, the sea stretched out towards the ocean.

"We need to land before we accidentally travel away from the Great Island, lest we end up in open sea—the great unknown sea," Ragnar said.

"Hmm, open sea certainly ain't what we need. We've already experienced sailing through the unknown. We can call ourselves lucky that we came to Pictland and didn't get entirely lost. But by Odin, now we need to land and not miss our chance!"

"We'll be able to get to Mercia by travelling across Cymry, if we dock at this place," I said. Ragnar nodded knowingly and steered nearer to the coast, while the others rowed with care and concentration. Something in me became excited as I realised that Mercia wasn't that far any more. The coast seemed uninhabited, apart from hundreds of seagulls. They circled above our heads, cooing and squawking and flying back and forth from the rocky coast, where hundreds more were residing. Rock after rock hindered us from docking at the coast, until a sandy, level patch turned up, enclosed by white rocks, opening up to a landscape of grassy, shrubby hills.

"Let's get ready for the great landing," Bard said, picking up on everyone's anticipation. We had now been travelling for six days, though it seemed much longer. I longed for stability, a place to stay, a home. And of course important questions revolved in my mind—and probably more so in Rohanna's. What had happened to our friends in Mercia? What was the year we were in? Were things the same as we had left them, or was everything going to be very different?

We dragged the boat with heaves and hoes onto the deserted land. Behind the tiny beach, the hills stretched on; and in the distance I spotted the beginning of a forest touching the horizon. There seemed to be no sign of a settlement nearby, not a soul to be seen. The men took the sail down and turned it into a tent. We made a small fire in front of the tent and ate the meat, bread and cheese from the Picts.

Olfi was back in his normal state, running around and discovering shells and stones on the beach. He was as free as a seagull and full of energy. Presenting some of his discoveries to Ljot, he asked pointing at the fire: "Won't strangers see the smoke and come over here?"

"That's a clever thought," Ljot praised him. "Yer not always safe to make a fire in the open." He cracked some more sticks and threw them into the crackling flames. "But a fire will keep wild animals away, if there are any."

"What kind of animals?" Olfi asked.

"Wolves, bears … who knows?"

There was just enough space for all twelve under the sail after we spread out our animal skins and wrapped ourselves in our hooded coats and blankets. The makeshift tent kept some of the wind out but didn't prevent cold and moisture, which made it almost like sleeping under the open sky. I found it hard to find sleep. When almost drifting off, some sound came from nature: a rustling in the shrubs, a strange animal cry, or someone getting up to add wood to the fire, or the baby crying; there was always something to prevent me from sleep. Eventually I got up in the middle of the night to leave the tent and gaze up at the stars. There were so many of them, sparkling innocently. I wondered how many past generations of people had gazed at them, just like me. Even though time passed and history constantly changed, these heavenly spots of light always remained the same. Generations before me and generations after me all had something in common—they had all existed and would exist under the very same stars. At some point in history, even in prehistoric times, someone else must have stood under the sky like me, filled with wonder and admiration for the inexplicable infinity of the universe. There were things in life such as this that we would never fully understand.

The others seemed to have found sleep, as regular breathing and snoring sounds mixed into a soundscape. The fire was low, so I added a few twigs and blew into the embers. The fire lit up anew, licking greedily at the wood.

Wales was next to England, but would it take a day or several days to get to Hamberton? Were we at the top, the middle or the bottom of the land they called Cymry? We needed to find out where Hamberton was, because

Durwyn's village would not be far from there. I knew that Hamberton was on the same level as South Wales. Hamberton didn't exist in the modern world, but it lay where the sea merges into the land, and becomes the River Severn. In our modern world, which we had left behind, that was also the area where the village lay in which we grew up. Durwyn's village was where we arrived after getting lost during our first arrival in Mercia—all those many years ago. At least it had been many years in our world... How many years or decades had passed in Mercia since then?

I looked up at the stars again. If they could see and think like people, they'd know everything. They have been there for thousands, millions of years. How little I knew, as a human ... how short my time was on earth, even though I was fortunate to cross time and history. I snuck back into the tent. Everyone appeared to be asleep. I lay down, unable to switch off my thoughts.

But I must eventually have fallen asleep, because I woke after sunrise to the twittering of birds hopping around the grass and the shrubs.

Chapter Fourteen—St Dewi's

During breakfast we decided to find some inhabitants. We had to get in contact with people who lived in the area in order to find out where we were exactly, how far from Mercia and how to get there. Would our food and water, the provisions the Picts had given us, last? Bard and Ragnar decided that a few of us should walk inland, and not stop until they'd reach a settlement.

"It may not be easy," Ragnar said between bites of oatmeal flatbread. "People are afraid of us. They expect us to raid and destroy."

Bard patted my shoulder with a heavy hand. "Adrian, our good man, you need to go with—perhaps you will be able to talk their language." He turned to his sons and commanded: "Erik, Bjorn and also Karl—you go along with Adrian. Together you'll be safe and strong. By Odin, who knows how these Cymry people might be? They could be the opposite of those generous Picts, bloodthirsty devils who'd want to pay revenge. Who knows?"

Ragnar wiped the crumbs off his tunic. "They won't be expecting much good from us strangers. Not after Vikings have been raiding before us! When you approach a settlement," Ragnar said, "first thing to say: the benefit of the gods be with you! We come in friendship and seek nothing else than advice."

Leaving the sea behind us, Erik, Bjorn, Karl and I stomped through the tough grass with shrubs scratching our legs. For a while the land sloped upwards so that we were soon able to look down to the sea and spot our boat standing in the pale sand looking like a little toy from this distance, and the rocky shores like bread crust. We strode on for about half an hour or more. There were no trees, nothing growing taller than the shrubs, and so we were able to see far ahead. Then something grey appeared in the distance, looking like a building.

"There's something like a fort," Bjorn exclaimed. "Perhaps they're watching us from there already…"

As we came closer, we discovered a long wall of round grey stones forming a circle around a couple of small buildings, of which we could just see the rooftops.

"Maybe they're crouching behind look-outs preparing to shoot us with bows and arrows," Karl suggested.

"Don't you think they'd give us a chance to speak first?" Erik asked.

"What do I know? *We* may not wanna fight, but them people could be ruffians," said Bjorn.

The wall was around two metres high, to the left of which were one or two fields of crops and behind it a slope with three or four cattle grazing. One of the buildings behind the wall was higher than the others. The roof was covered with thin black slates, and the top part of the stone tower had a few tiny windows—or rather gaps—between the stones. By the look of it, it might have been a fort and there might have been weaponed watchers behind each spyhole. From afar we couldn't tell if anyone was there or not, and I wondered how near we should approach the site. This wasn't a village, but the place was inhabited by people—you could tell that by the animals, the crops, the fields, but there wasn't anybody around. The closer we got, the easier it would be to shoot at us from those little windows. From this distance we were defenceless, since we had no shields; we carried just a sword each for close-up fighting. Single seagulls soared above the grey walls of the building, letting out an occasional cry. Apart from that, the place was strangely silent. Were there any people present? Were they out for the day, or were they spying on us at this very moment?

"Shall we carry on?" Bjorn asked. We were about 100 m away. The encircling wall had one place of entry: a rounded wooden door with an iron lock.

"If they'd wanted to shoot at us, they'd have done it by now, don't ye think?" Erik said.

"Yeah, but if they charge us from close up, we have the upper hand. After all, nobody's known to be better fighters than us…" Karl, Erik and Bjorn stepped on, their hands on their swords, ready to pull them out if necessary. Even though I thought we could easily be overpowered by those who might be behind the walls of this building, there was something in the air, something in this place that didn't radiate anything aggressive. In fact it would have surprised me if an aggressor leapt out from that door or jumped up on the wall. The place seemed calm and quiet. The only thing that was missing was people. The cattle and sheep didn't care about the four of us approaching—as if they were used to strangers turning up.

This was the only settlement, as far as our eyes could see, so we had to give it a try. Karl went up to the door and banged on it.

"No one answering … go in?" Erik asked. As soon as he had said so, Bjorn opened the door and we snuck into the enclosed space. In front of us were rows of vegetable beds and all sorts of herbs enriching the air with spicy scents. This instantly took me back to the small monastery in Hamberton, only here the vegetable beds weren't arranged in a circle, they ran along the wall and some plants were growing up the walls, including fruit trees. Apart from a few small stone buildings, there were little wooden huts probably used as workshops. The larger stone building was shaped like a horseshoe, and in its middle was soft grass, cut short, and rose bushes.

"This place seems deserted, but at the same time it is inhabited," Erik whispered, pointing at the well-kept garden.

"Maybe ghosts live here," Bjorn whispered, without smiling. He was serious.

"Let's help ourselves to some apples," Karl said. We were hungry and the ripe apples so close at hand were tempting.

"Not so greedy, man," Erik hissed. "Someone might jump out at us from a hiding place... We've gotta stay alert, for Odin's sake!"

We approached the grey horseshoe building, and Karl banged on the door. Once again, there was no answer. We looked at each other, puzzled. Should we leave this place or enter without permission? Erik gave a nod and Karl opened the door. Inside it was quite dark, with a smell of cool stone and wood as we stepped in. Our feet echoed on the bare stone floor. There were doors left and right, all closed. We walked to the end of the corridor, and carried on around the corner. Sunlight beamed in through a window, creating a square of light on the floor. There were more doors left and right, but then the corridor ended at a large double door where we all stopped, not knowing what we'd find behind it. This time Karl knocked gently on the door, but again no one answered. He slowly pushed it open, then held his breath. We joined him to see what was inside. There was a large space with a row of windows along one side with sunlight pouring in. In the centre of the hall, two dozen men in grey hooded cloaks knelt in front of a cross, mumbling, their heads bent in prayer. The one in the front shot up when he heard us entering. He was alert, but unarmed.

"The peace of the gods be with you!" Erik called out. "Fear not, we are not going to do you any harm!" His voice echoed on the bare walls. I hoped the men wouldn't mistake this for an attack. They wouldn't understand what he had announced in Norse. I rapidly translated into

English, hoping they'd understand my language. Some heads turned, their eyes fixed on us. I saw in their expression a mix of anxiety, mildness and pity. Some remained bent in prayer. The standing man pushed his hood back. He had short light brown hair, fair skin and grey-blue eyes like the colour of the sea. He strode over towards us.

"What do you seek? Aren't you Vikings, men of the North?" he asked in English with an unfamiliar accent. I translated what he said.

"Yes, we are!" Erik answered. "We are Norsemen who've come from across the sea. We live in the mountainous country of the Norse. At sea we've been attacked by monsters and got lost. But we found refuge among the Picts, then travelled south."

The monk looked us up and down. He observed us holding our swords and seemed to question whether we were a threat or not.

"Why do you come here to our monastery?" he asked.

"All we need is some advice and food. We are stranded not far from here. We want to travel to Mercia. We have come to start a new life there," Erik continued.

"You have not come to raid and cause terror?" the monk asked, his eyebrows raised.

"Nay, friend. We're here to seek your help."

"How many are there apart from you? Is there a whole battalion?"

I shook my head and told him there were only a dozen of us, including women and children. The monk exhaled. "We have seen you approaching through the look-out. We gathered here in our chapel to pray, because we were expecting an attack. As you see—we are unarmed. In the last days we have heard of Viking raids where no life is spared. Thus, we prepared for our own end." He turned to his fellow monks and spoke in a low voice to them as they all surrounded him. There was some exchange and gesticulating, but I didn't hear what they said. It didn't last long, then the leader of the monks told them to leave the chapel and invited us to follow.

One after the other genuflected before the cross in the centre, then silently left the room. They dipped their fingertips in a bowl of water, crossed themselves from the forehead down to the chest, and escorted us away from the chapel. We entered a hall with long tables and benches. It was dinner time and all the monks were talking as they sat down at the tables.

"I'm Dewi. You are very welcome to dine with us," the leader said.

The air was filled with the smell of cooked vegetables, which made my stomach grumble. I remembered that I hadn't had anything cooked for days, and it seemed like ages since I had sat at a table for a meal.

Chapter Fifteen—Dinner with the Monks

When all the monks were gathered at the tables, they stood up for a short prayer of thanksgiving and a blessing, then sat down again. Erik, Karl, Bjorn and I sat among the monks. A chunky vegetable soup was ladled into wooden bowls and slices of dark bread were placed next to each bowl. One of the monks poured water into handleless mugs for us to drink.

While we ate our soup, no one spoke apart from a monk who sat separately opposite the long tables and read from a large book, which must have been a Bible.

Erik, Bjorn, Karl and I began gobbling our soup, but when I looked up I noticed that the monks were eating slowly and mindfully. If we carried on like this we would finish our soup much sooner than they, and then we'd have to sit there feeling embarrassed.

"Slow down a bit," I mumbled to the others. "We needn't hurry!"

Erik, sitting next to me, looked up and realised what I meant. He gave the others a nod to slow down.

"No meat in this…" Bjorn mumbled, and I was glad the monks didn't understand Norse.

"Well, guess why these men are so slim," Erik added.

"Stop being rude," Karl grumbled as he gobbled on.

Even though we tried to slow down, we were finished before the monks. Then one of them stood up and went to the kitchen, returning with a dish of four fried fish and more bread.

"May I give you some?" he said. "This fish comes from the sea nearby." We happily accepted. He placed in each of our four emptied bowls a roasted fish and bread. But the monks, once they'd finished their soup, ate no more. So the fish was solely for us guests! Crispy and buttery on the outside and juicy on the inside, seasoned with salt and herbs, it was the most delicious fish I had ever eaten.

While we dined—humbled by our privilege—the monks held light conversation until we were finished. Then they all stood up and another prayer of thanks was said before most of them left the dining hall. Dewi joined us and asked how they could be of help.

"I'm still wondering why he and his men weren't prepared for an attack, why they were unarmed," Karl said. Before I decided whether I should translate this, Dewi asked what Karl had asked; so I told him that we were all surprised to see them kneeling in prayer rather than getting ready to defend themselves.

"Oh, well," Dewi began, "we had seen you approaching from afar. But as monks, rather than wanting to fight, we rely on God's protection. We hand over everything to God's will. That is why we gathered in the chapel to pray, ready to face our fate in whatever way."

"Do ye not possess any arms at all?" Erik asked.

"Why should we? No. We don't have weapons. Though you could say that our strongest weapon against evil is prayer. We have learned from our Lord not to hit back if an enemy hits us. Instead, we remain peaceful and even bless our enemies."

Erik shook his head in disbelief as I translated.

"Yer lucky we've come in peace. But what yer gonna do when raiders come? How can ye just kneel and pray when yer being attacked? What ye gonna do without sword and spear?"

"We'll do the same," Dewi answered with a smile on his face that was free from all doubts.

"But surely ye don't want yer men to suffer death? You could defend yerself before anyone approaches yer wall! The look-outs in the tower are good for that, ain't they?"

Dewi shook his head. "We are not here to exercise violence. The way we prayed when you came is what we'd do, even if another time it might be raiders. We feared an attack, and we expected that more men would turn up."

"I don't think raiders would spare ye, if yer on yer knees," Erik continued.

"Yes, that may be so. But we would pray for the souls of our attackers."

"They'll cut you in pieces!"

"Then we'd die a martyr's death," Dewi said, looking down to the ground. "Martyrdom is the greatest honour we can get on earth, if it means to die for our Lord, for the truth, for faith. The blood of a martyr is the seed of faith that grows in others. Our Lord died for us, so why shouldn't we die for him? He died innocently and perfect in holiness … whereas we are nowhere near his state of perfection."

"Who, by Odin, is this Lord yer talking about?" Erik asked.

"Jesus Christ is our Lord," Dewi answered and bowed his head in respect as he said so.

I noticed that the other monk who was clearing the table, taking away the stacked bowls and spoons, also bowed when he heard the name of Christ.

"So what are your plans?" Dewi then asked as we left the dining hall. "You want to go to Mercia?"

"My sister and I are originally from England … I mean from Mercia, and we are helping these Vikings to find a new home," I explained.

"Your Viking friends will have to learn the language of the Angles," he said. Erik nodded in agreement when I told him. "I've already begun picking up some bits," he said.

"What kind of place is this?" he asked. "Why do you live together like this, yet there are no wives and children?"

I translated Erik's question. "Yes, he's right," the monk answered. "We don't marry and we don't have our own family. Or perhaps you could say that living in brotherhood is like a family. We are dedicated to a life of chastity, thus we are completely free to serve God. Our main duty is to pray and work (*ora et labora* we call it in Latin) and to help and educate the poor."

"Which god do you pray to?" Bjorn asked.

"There is only one God, and we pray to him."

"Only one God? This is like with the Picts," Bjorn remembered. "What's the name of your God?"

"God is Father, but also God the Son—that is Christ," he answered. Bjorn, Karl and Erik looked at the monk, puzzled.

"So, there *are* two Gods after all?" Erik asked.

The monk shook his head. "God the Father, God the Son and God the Holy Spirit…"

"So, there are *three*," Karl interrupted.

The monk shook his head again. "No, my friends. There's only one God. But he is the Holy Trinity. One God —three persons." We followed him outside where he suddenly bent down and picked a shamrock that was growing in the grass.

"See this shamrock?" he asked. We all nodded. (Erik, Karl and Bjorn repeated the word 'shamrock', eager to learn English.) "Do you see how it has three parts?"

"Yes," we said.

"Three parts, but it's still one plant, do you see?"

"Yes…"

"It's the same with God: One God, but three persons: Father, Son and Holy Spirit."

"I get that God can also appear as a Spirit—but how can he be a Father and a Son at the same time? That's more than any of our Gods can perform…" Erik said, stroking his plaited beard.

The monk nodded and said we should follow him again. He led us back to the horseshoe building, to a room where six of the monks were each leaning over a large book with empty pages; they held a feather in their hand which they dipped into a pot of ink to scribe elegant words. Set up in front of each was another large book from which they copied words and sentences into the book on their desk.

"See this book?" Dewi asked, indicating one of them. The monk who was writing in it looked up briefly and greeted us with a smile and a nod. On the left page of his book, the first letter of the sentence stood out: it was large and beautifully decorated with red, blue, green and yellow swirls, figures, saints and animals. I gasped in awe, admiring the skill of such hand-painted art, and it was hard to take my eyes off it.

"This is the Bible, the Holy Scripture. In the Bible you can read God's word," Dewi explained. "We are just at the place where it says that God sent his own Son into the world. It was God himself. He was born as a baby—a human. You see, God wanted to be close to us, and he wanted us to understand him better. That's why he came down to Earth. God is Father and Son at the same time."

"Who gave birth to this God?" Erik asked.

"It was the blessed Virgin Mary. She was chosen to give birth to our Saviour."

"Saviour?" Bjorn asked. "Why do you call him a Saviour? Is he the one that saved us at sea?"

The grey-eyed monk smiled. "He most probably did! But more importantly, Christ saves our souls…"

"He has come to save all mankind; he is the Way, the Truth and the Life." Each time Dewi spoke Jesus' name, the monks stopped writing and bowed their heads.

"What does that cross in the other room mean?" Erik asked, pointing in the direction of the chapel.

"The cross reminds us that Jesus died for us. He was crucified, which was a kind of punishment, even though he was without sin. That took place over seven hundred years ago."

"Are you saying your God was killed? But isn't your God immortal? Surely a God doesn't die…!" Erik exclaimed.

"Yes, you're right. Jesus was killed, but he was also resurrected from the dead. He became alive again, on the third day after his death—he had conquered death! After that he rose into Heaven, but He's also with us, always."

Chapter Sixteen—The Monastery

"It's afternoon," Dewi declared. "This is the time for work, but I can show you around the monastery if you'd like to."

"Oh, yes!" Erik, Bjorn and Karl eagerly agreed. There wasn't a hurry to get back to the camp. First he led us to the garden, pointing out the cabbage, onions, leek, carrots, parsley, peppermint and many other herbs growing in neat rows and patches. There were berry bushes (the berries were already over) and apple, pear and quince trees where the fruit would soon be ripe for harvesting. A monk drew water from a well in a leather bucket as Dewi explained: "This is where it all began…"

"What began here?" Erik asked.

"It was a miracle—the water. It started here as a spring. People noticed they were getting healed miraculously. Some were blind and could see again, one was crippled and could walk again, and it is even said that a young boy, thought to be dead, came back to live. Many people have been healed and possibly many more converted."

"How was the spring discovered?" Bjorn asked.

"According to what has been passed on orally (we have now written the story down), around 200 years ago there was a holy woman who had seen an apparition; she was told in her dream that if she went to this place, she'd come across a spring with blessed water and that place should become a monastery where men would live in modesty and chastity, following in the footsteps of the saints."

Dewi then led us to a workshop where a couple of monks were crafting small items of wood, and another workshop where two monks were shaping bowls out of wet clay. There was also a stone oven where one monk was kneading dough while another was removing bread from the oven and stacking the loaves in a basket. "It smells so good, doesn't it?" Dewi said. "This batch will last for five days."

"How many monks are there to feed?" Karl asked.

"There are 24 brothers, but we also bake bread for guests and the poor."

"How often do you have visitors?" I asked as we headed back to the long grey building.

"We often have pilgrims coming to see the well and to pray; there are a few every week, especially during the warm season. In winter it is usually quieter. But even then we still have people visiting, sometimes high-ranking people and others who seek advice and spiritual guidance," he said, opening the door. "And there are always the poor asking for alms…"

As we entered the building, Karl asked: "So, who started this way of life?"

"Oh, yes. I need to tell you of Saint David. He founded this monastery, and several more throughout the British Isles. He was a holy man, full of love for God and the people. He performed several miracles and is now in heaven, that's why we call him a saint." Dewi stopped to make the sign of the cross.

"So was he a kind of a half-god?" Bjorn asked.

"Oh, no, no. Not at all! As I mentioned earlier, there is only one God and no others besides him. No half-gods either. But God uses holy men to do holy things in his name. The place here is named after this saint: Saint David's."

"Did he die recently?" Karl asked.

Dewi shook his head. "Saint David died 200 years ago, God bless his soul... He was aged 147 when his life on earth ended."

"That old?" I asked, perplexed. Dewi continued: "Yes, not all of us will reach such a good age... Saint David's last words were: 'Stay joyful, keep the faith and the credo, do the little things the way I showed you.' After his death his fellow monks and also people from all around fasted for three days. Saint David established twelve monasteries across the country. And till today, we follow his holy footsteps and try to live like him and convert others to the true faith."

We arrived at the chapel again. Dewi opened the door and let us enter ahead of him. He genuflected and made the sign of the cross, while focusing on the decorated cross in the centre. After a short moment of silence he whispered: "This is where we spend three hours of the day and three hours of the night."

"By Odin, why do you spend so much time in this hall...?" asked Bjorn, looking around at the rather empty space. Apart from the cross and benches, there were a row of windows letting in the sunlight and two statues of saints to the side. In front of the cross was an altar covered with a white cloth and three unlit candles at each end. Above the altar, in front of the cross was a cube-shaped tabernacle covered with a white cloth embroidered with gold thread.

"We pray, sing and meditate here," Dewi replied. "It's the most important of all we do, you see." Then he walked with us along the walls around the chapel and pointed out 13 small crosses hanging on the walls. "Each one of these represents the passion of Christ—what he suffered from the moment he was condemned to death." Back at the altar, he said: "The candle light reminds us of Christ's glory and his triumph over death." Before leaving the chapel, Dewi genuflected and bowed again, and my Viking friends and I followed suit. What else could we do than show some kind of respect towards what was holy for our hosts?

We left the garden through a small back gate. In front of us was a field where three monks were ploughing the earth. They weren't using a horse or an ox to plough; instead, one of the monks was pulling the plough himself, using all his strength while bending over. The two other brothers were helping him by leading the plough in the desired direction.

"Not so long ago, we harvested barley, and now these brothers are preparing the earth for the next sowing."

"Don't you have animals to do this job?" Erik asked, staring at the monk toiling with the plough. "It would be much easier with an ox to pull the plough!"

"Following Saint David's example, we need to work hard, you see. We feel the work is better done with our own hands. It is good for us, it humbles us…"

"I hope you get enough to eat each day," Bjorn replied. "For this type of work, you must be eating lots."

"Depending on how much physical work he does and also on his body, a monk will get the nutrition he needs. We usually have one meal a day."

"Only one meal a day?" Karl asked with wide eyes.

"Yes, one meal; and like today, sometimes we share this meal with guests."

"What do you usually drink—do you brew mead with the barley you grow?"

"No, we don't drink mead. Water, just plain water. It's good enough and it's all we need."

When we arrived back at the garden, a man appeared at the gate asking for bread for his family. Then a woman with a small basket came to pick herbs. The monk who assisted her asked how the person who required the herbs was doing—I assumed it was her husband—and she replied that he was recovering fast. The monk promised to pray for him. Then as soon as she left someone else approached with a similar request for a certain plant. The monks attended their visitors with patience and politeness. When they handed out the bread and herbs, they gave blessings and made the sign of the cross over the person or over whatever they handed out.

Soon after that, a humble-looking stooped man arrived with three fair-haired children. One of the monks handed each some bread and leeks, and each child replied with a clear: "Thank you, father," and "God bless you!" As they left, another woman arrived and sat down on a small wooden bench under an apple tree for a brief conversation with a monk.

"Are your men some kind of druids, that people come to seek your help and advice?" Erik asked.

Dewi answered: "Not druids, we are monks. We have chosen to live a life of poverty, chastity and obedience."

"What is chastity?"

"It means we don't marry, we don't have a wife or a girlfriend. We choose to live abstinently all our life long."

"And poverty? Why on earth would you chose to live poor?" Bjorn asked, bewildered. And when I translated, Dewi answered, "It's because nothing on earth is as great as in heaven. We live poorly so that we can be closer to heaven."

"Crazy men," Erik mumbled, shaking his head, but there was something admiring in his voice.

About an hour had passed since Dewi had shown us around. "We must go back to the camp!" Erik suddenly exclaimed. We had been so enraptured with the monastery and the life here, we'd almost forgotten about the world outside, the camp where the others were waiting for us and the journey to Mercia in front of us.

"Could you give us the directions to Mercia?" Erik asked. "How far is it still?"

"Ah, yes of course, Mercia! Which place in Mercia are you heading to?" Dewi asked.

"Do you know Hamberton?" I asked.

"I might have heard of it," he said, narrowing his eyebrows. "You won't be able to enter Mercia by land, though."

"Why?" I asked. "We aren't that far, are we?"

"That's not the problem. It is a two-day walk to Mercia from here. But you will not be able to cross the border so easily, since King Offa has built a wall along the border. Have you not heard of Offa's dyke?"

I shook my head, but perhaps I had a faint memory from history about the dyke.

"Does the dyke run all along Cymry?"

"Yes, King Offa is so terrified of the Cymry people, he built a wall to protect Mercia, and you won't be able to pass through. It is better to travel by water in order to get to Mercia unhindered. There is a bay that runs into Mercia and turns into the River Severn; I believe Hamberton is in that area."

"That means more travelling on water…" I said to the others. But they didn't seem to be bothered.

When it was time to say goodbye, some of the monks gathered around us. "I like it here," Karl announced. "Could we come back another time?" One of the monks who kept smiling answered: "I think we're going to see you again!"

"Well, who knows… Tristan has predicted things ahead, more than once!" Dewi said, nodding at the other monk.

"I think God has great plans for you," Tristan continued, pointing at Erik's chest.

"We love great things," Erik boasted.

"But we have to go back to the camp. I bet they're getting worried about us," Bjorn said, stretching out both arms and nudging his brother's and Karl's backs.

"Bring them some bread," Dewi told one of the monks, whom I remembered seeing at the bread oven, "and fish!" he ordered to another.

Each of us gave Dewi a hug. It was as if we were friends who had known each other a long time. As we left the monastery we carried two large sacks filled with bread, fish and cheese and some leeks. It made us feel rich—this would last for days! There was also something in our hearts which had made us richer—hard to explain.

"There's something about these men," Erik broke the silence as we strode through the wild grass.

"Are you impressed by them?" Karl asked.

"I guess so. I don't think I've ever met such … what shall I say—peaceful, happy people," Erik said.

"They hardly possess anything," Bjorn said, "and yet they seemed so pleased."

"How do they do it?"

"It must be from praying. Their God is powerful—they don't even fear death."

"Praying instead of fighting," Erik mumbled, shaking his head in disbelief.

"Can you imagine leading a life like that?" Bjorn asked.

"Are you mad?" Erik answered.

Soon we were admiring the view of the sea again. It wouldn't be far to the camp from here. I suddenly felt excited and energised. Was it because I was young again, or was I anticipating something that was ahead of us? It wasn't just me. Karl and the two brothers stretched out their arms in the breeze and began jumping over shrubs. We hadn't been out on land for days before arriving here, but it was also as if something had awoken in us, filling us with hope and new energy.

"Hey," Karl shouted. "Let's race!" All four began running, laughing, shouting and skipping like young deer in spring.

Chapter Seventeen—Back at the Camp

Ragnar and Bard watched us with arms folded and Helga with hands on hips as we arrived back at the camp.

"By Odin, where have ye been all this time?" Helga cried out as soon as we were within earshot.

"It's all right, it's all right," Erik calmed her down. "We've found out all we need to know, and nothing has happened to us."

Rohanna came up to me. "This was getting terribly boring," she whispered. "Are we now in Wales? What did you find out?"

"Yes, it is Wales," I answered. "Cymry, they call it. Remember? But we're not going to get to England by land…"

"We *are* going there, aren't we?" she asked, worried.

"We will, we will. I believe it's not that far, but we'll have to travel by boat."

"Was it far to the first settlement in this area?" Bard asked.

"Tell us what kept you so long away…" Ragnar said, looking us up and down.

"It's been so long since ye all left!" Helga said. "Now, tell us the news."

"Oh, it's not how you all imagine," Erik said, shaking his head.

"Go on then, tell us, whom have ye met?" Bard asked.

"We've met unusual people. They called themselves … what was it again?"

"Monks," I said.

"Yes, monks. A group of 24 men living together—working and praying. They had no wives nor children."

"They don't have family?" Helga asked.

"Nay, and they also choose to own little, yet they have enough to help others."

"So, what did these men tell ye?"

"They gave us food," Bjorn said, and Karl opened the sacks to show off the contents.

"That's a lot of good-looking food," Helga said, mighty pleased.

"That will keep us going for days," Ragnar agreed. "Now, how far are we from the Mercia kingdom and how do we get there?"

"The monks explained that it's better to go by ship," I explained. "There's a dyke all along the border between Cymry and Mercia, and soldiers are guarding it. The monks said it would be impossible to get through. But if we travel by sea, we should come to a bay where the River Severn cuts into the land; this river would bring us near Hamberton."

"Well, we've got all we need for the next few days. Let's pack up and get on the ship!" Bard announced.

It took us half an hour to pack and sort things on the boat. Karl, Bjorn and Bard pulled the sail up, and with heave-hoes we pushed the boat back into the water until it was afloat. With the wooden decking under my feet, the sea air blowing in my face and the forever rocking water, it soon felt like home again. Ragnar took his place at the rudder and the rest of us sat at an oar to make our way along the coast, but not too close to the reefs where the water smacked against bare rock.

The weather changed constantly. One moment the sky was covered with grey clouds, then they scattered apart letting the sun strike down and warm the boat. A constant wind moved the clouds across the sun anew, and it even rained a little, but only for a minute or two.

Our fellow travellers begged Rohanna and me to teach them some basic words and first sentences in our native language. Out on the sea with little distraction and little to do, learning was swift and straightforward. Eager as they were, they'd soon be communicating with the basic phrases needed for everyday life.

After hours of travelling along the rocky coast, the shoreline changed into wide sandy beaches, and in the distance we sometimes saw small buildings and smoke rising to the sky. We travelled on until a bay opened up with two small islands and the coast visible on both sides. A river ran out into the sea from the bay—a spate of dark green fresh water flowing into the grey-blue of the sea.

"We'd better not go up the river—there will be more settlements on the river's side, and we'd be exposed to attacks," Bard said.

"I'm keeping me eyes open for a spot to land," Ragnar said. "Shouldn't be difficult—there aren't any rocks, just green everywhere. The grass spills into the bay. Look at it —full of vegetation. This is the kind of place we've been longing for, folks!"

Further off the coast there was forest. Not long after, Ragnar found a place to beach the boat, where we could hide it in the bushes. Eagerly we jumped into the water and pulled the boat onto the shore. Sticks floated in the water and trees were bent towards the river, their roots protruding in the water.

We pushed our way through a tangle of plants and bushes—some of us tugging and others pushing the boat onto land. Then we took out all the possessions we needed for the coming days and covered the boat with the sail, as if putting it to sleep.

"This is it!" said Bard, as we got ready to walk inland. "We've completed our voyage—and what a voyage it was!"

"Ah, but now another kind of voyage begins," said Helga. And she was right, for now our voyage would proceed on land. We could not know where it would take us, what things would happen, whom we'd meet and where we'd settle.

Chapter Eighteen—Back in Mercia

We all had baggage strapped on our backs as we began marching through the bushes. The march took us up a slope, which I hoped would overlook the area and help us determine where to go. It was hot weather, and the heat and strain slowed us down. Every tree we passed rescued us from the dazzling afternoon sun by providing shade before we trudged on upwards, panting and sweating. Just when I thought this was getting unbearable—the weight on my back dug my feet into the ground and my shoulders were aching—we reached the top of the hill. There were fewer bushes here, and our toil was rewarded with a panoramic view revealing settlements scattered on the hillsides and across the flat land.

From here I spotted a rather large settlement. "Isn't that…?"

Rohanna stood next to me and held her breath. "It's Hamberton!" she said, looking to the west with her hand shielding her eyes from the sun. "It's got to be Hamberton. See how it lies by the river? And there's a long stone building,surrounded by a wall—that's got to be the monastery. It all looks exactly how I remember it."

"That *is* Hamberton," I agreed. "There is no other settlement the size of a small town around here." I observed the villages scattered around the area. "One of them will be Durwyn's village," I announced. Rohanna didn't answer, but I could feel the tension in the air. We weren't far from the places we longed for … but we also weren't far from finding out what had happened to the people we had known. "If we go to Hamberton, from there we'll find our way to the village. And if we're not sure, we'll ask someone."

As the others joined us, I said to Bard: "Do you see that large settlement?" pointing across the hills. "If we go to that town, we're close to the place where we all could start a new life."

"Whatever," Bard exclaimed. "Bring us there, son, and we'll be glad. Ragnar, come and look!"

"Everyone, try to remember the direction. We need to follow the sun!" Ragnar said.

"Just you walk ahead," said Helga, "and we'll follow in single file."

"I'll need a couple of men with swords," said Ragnar. "Looks like thickets of bushes and thorns, and they'll need cutting to free the way."

He was right—the way downhill was densely covered with brushwood. The men went ahead with their swords, as if in battle, fighting their way through the tangle, whilst carrying the heavy packs on their backs. Sawing through the brambles of blackberry bushes, they gained bloody scratches on their hands and arms where their sleeves were rolled up. Sweat pearls appeared on their foreheads and their faces became red from the endeavour. I followed behind them with Helga, Rohanna, Astrid who carried the baby in a sling, and Ljot leading Olfi by the hand.

The sun was already setting and Hamberton was still far. We had been walking for about two hours, and we probably had another two hours in front of us. Because there was no road or path, everything took much longer. We had come to a clearing that was less overgrown—a flat space between a couple of rocks.

"This is a good place for a rest," Bard said as we all stopped to breathe out. "Perhaps we should stay here overnight, unless we reach the closest village before it's dark…"

"Camping is the only thing we can do," said Ragnar. "I don't think we'll get there before dark, and ain't no point carrying on after that. There's no moon today, either. And anyway, even if we reached the next village, who would want to take in strangers suddenly turning up at night? We can't expect to be lucky every time, as we were with the Picts and the minks…"

"You mean the monks," Erik said.

"Yeh, them monks, whatever. Down in the villages people will be suspicious of strangers—can't blame them. We'd better send Adrian and his sister on their own in the morning. They can talk to the villagers, find out how things are, whether we're welcome to settle in or if we ain't welcome at all."

"I'm sure they gonna be open-minded; after all, we ain't doing them any harm," Bjorn said, leaning on one of the rocks and chewing on a blade of grass.

"But that's not a guarantee that they gonna love us. I think it's better we stop off here in the wilderness. We can stay for several days … it won't do us any harm to have a break from travelling," Ragnar said.

"I like the idea of staying in one place for once. What do you think, Astrid?" Helga asked. Astrid produced a tired smile. "Yeah, I don't mind having a break from travelling…"

"The weather is warm, no rain in prospect—we should build a shelter!" Bard announced. He pointed over to the forest which began close to where we rested. "There will be plenty of branches and twigs to find there. We'll need a very long branch and several short ones, to start off with."

With that, Bjorn, Karl, Ljot and Erik went off to get branches: one about 10 metres long, and at its thickest part about 30 cm wide. I helped them to secure it at an angle in the ground. Bard had dug a hole and we pushed stones underneath to stabilize it. The branch was supported at its other end by a shorter, sturdy branch which Ragnar hit into the ground with help of a stone. All of us then collected thinner branches and sticks which we leant against the big branch. To finish off the shelter we put layers of fern and other leafy plants on top of the twigs. In the end it looked like a roof standing on the ground. It took about two hours to complete, and I was quite proud of the results of our work. The shelter may not have been as sturdy as a house, but it would protect us from wind and rain. As an architect, for most of my life (in the other world) I had been designing homes and other constructions, but I had never accomplished a shelter of natural materials within just a couple of hours.

"Wouldn't it be good to have a fire in case there're wild animals roaming around here?" I asked.

"Of course! But we lost all the equipment for making a fire at sea, during the monster attacks," Bard reminded us.

Ragnar investigated the ground. "This might do," he said, picking up a black piece of rock. "It's firestone!"

"Oh, it's flint," I said, touching the sharp edges.

"Yes, very useful for tools and for sparking a fire!" Karl said. He picked up two other flint stones and began hitting them against each other until tiny sparks jumped off the stone. Ljot held some dry leaves under the sparks, and after several attempts the leaves caught fire. Bjorn cleared a patch on the ground and added more leaves and dry twigs and bark, and soon we had a proper fire going. Rohanna and I watched over the fire and fed it with more wood, while Bard and the three young men went hunting in the thicket.

"I wonder what they'll come back with?" I said.

"There could be deer in the forest." Rohanna answered. But after about an hour they came back with nothing.

We settled by the fire, ate our leftovers and were chatting about plans for future homes when Ragnar, who had been quiet, suddenly said: "Hush, everyone!" He crawled away from the fire and hid behind a bush.

Everyone was silent until we suddenly heard a grunting sound. Then everything happened quickly: Ragnar hit out with his sword. Loud squeals and grunting noises came from behind another bush, and then sudden silence. Ragnar returned to the fire, dragging a dead animal with black bristles. It was a large boar! Ragnar and Bard skinned the animal and began cutting it apart, taking out the intestines. The others didn't seem to mind the slaughter, but Rohanna and I both turned away.

"Let's go for a walk," Rohanna suggested, tugging my sleeve. She didn't like seeing blood and had turned pale. I feared she might pass out, so quickly followed her.

"We're going to look for some berries," I told the others.

"Take this for the berries," Helga said, throwing a cloth to Rohanna in which she could collect the fruit. "And don't get lost!" she shouted after us.

When we were out of earshot, Rohanna sighed. Now we had the opportunity to speak about our concerns, what had been lingering in our minds.

"Don't you sometimes think," she began, "that we might have come back to Mercia for a new reason? Perhaps we'll never see those people we knew before…"

And I wondered if she was right. But how could she accept having waited all her life for Durwyn? I didn't want to discourage her with this question, so I shook my head and answered:

"There's no need to think that way … I mean, we can't guarantee anything, but tomorrow's the big day—at least the big day for us! We will find out all we need to know. First thing in Hamberton, I'll ask if the monastery still exists; and if it does, then we'll go there and see if we recognise the same monks, and they'll tell us what year this is. From that we'll be able to draw a conclusion."

We strolled on through the trees, not really looking for berries, but we did come across some. Tangles of raspberries and blackberries were growing in a sunny clearing, so Rohanna picked some to taste.

"Delicious, and so sweet!" she said. "Perhaps I'm only imagining it, but these berries taste far better than the ones we used to buy in the supermarket."

"*Used* to?" I asked with curious surprise.

"Well, you know, back in the other world. Why so surprised?"

"Oh, it just sounded strange, as if … as if that life was over, and we wouldn't go back to it."

Rohanna paused in picking berries. "Well, who knows…" she muttered. "What if we never *do* go back this time…"

Rohanna placed the cloth on the ground and we heaped our raspberries and blackberries in it. Then she carefully picked up the ends and twisted them in a knot. Then we headed back to camp.

The scrumptious smell of roasting meat reached our noses even before we saw the camp. Next to the fire lay the remains of the boar, and sitting round the fire were Bard and Ljot roasting chunks of meat on sticks over the flames. It sizzled as grease dripped into the fire. When the meat was ready, Helga cut it in pieces with a dagger and we consumed the meat on barley bread from the monks. The sky darkened and the stars twinkled. Ragnar started singing a song, and instead of playing instruments—they too had got lost at sea—he smacked his hands on his leg, as did Bard, Karl and the others. The tune had become familiar to us in the meantime. It was the same song they'd sung as we sailed down the fjords in Norway. But now they sang more quietly—perhaps for fear of being heard by the inhabitants of this, for them, strange country. I hummed along with the tune as I lay on my back, my arms folded under my head, gazing into the endless universe, and once again admiring the stars.

What was awaiting us tomorrow? I couldn't tell, but I would accept whichever way it turned out. There was no point in holding on to my own ideas. How could I know what was best for Rohanna and me? If things turned out differently from what we wanted, there was nothing else we could do but accept our fate.

When the fire died down to a glow, we all retreated under the shelter. I lay down in the very back corner, where the space between roof and ground was the shallowest. On each side of the shelter were five grown-ups, while the two children lay between their parents. Space was scarce, and as someone's feet would touch someone else's head and someone's head would touch someone else's feet, people complained and grunted. "We should build at least one more shelter tomorrow," someone suggested. "Or better three or four," another replied, annoyed. Perhaps they were right. Who knew for how long this was going to be our temporary home? What if nobody welcomed us into their village community?

I fell asleep with these thoughts, and didn't wake until early morning when flocks of birds were tweeting and chirruping at daybreak as the first sunlight appeared above the horizon.

Rohanna was up already and had left the shelter.

We washed our faces with water from the skin bottles we still had from the Picts. Rohanna combed her hair with a comb she had received from a Pict woman, and tied it into two plaits, which made her look even younger. She brushed her clothes and scrubbed off stains that had come from travelling for days. She was obviously concerned about her appearance and was preparing herself for whoever we were to meet. Following her example, I pulled my clothes straight and flattened the creases on my sleeves and trouser legs.

After eating a little meat and bread for breakfast, we left the group and headed downhill. The morning was fresh, and as we walked through the knee-high vegetation, our clothes grew damp from the dew. Then gradually the sun rose and the air became warmer and stuffier. It was going to be another hot summer's day.

Chapter Nineteen—Hamberton Market

The way downhill was less overgrown with bushes and thorns (otherwise we couldn't have got through without a knife or sword) and it led away from the forest. Soon we reached a man-made path, and I felt a rush of excitement. This was the path that would lead us back to Hamberton! So many years, even decades, had passed and now we were almost back—back to the place we'd loved and missed all this time. Durwyn's village would be an hour's walk away from Hamberton. But first we had to answer the most important question: Were we going to meet our old friends, or had we arrived in a completely different time?

Rohanna had become quiet, though inside she must have been nervous. The air was hot and she rolled her sleeves back. I noticed that her fingers trembled, and she flipped her hair back nervously. We kept stopping in the shade of the trees growing along the stony path. I too was nervous, even though I had less reason to be so. Unlike her, I hadn't been waiting for someone else all my life. I had been married for a great part of my life. Rohanna had forgone that opportunity several times because, as it seemed, she had already given her heart away to Durwyn. Now we were close to finding out whether this had been for a good reason, or for nothing. The matter was complicated and yet so simple.

After following the path for around half an hour, we saw the walls and rooftops of Hamberton rising in front of us. Every step brought us closer to the reality which would soon reveal itself. We didn't talk any more, just walked on, each immersed in our own thoughts. The closer we came to the little town, the more people came by: some were carrying baskets filled with vegetables and fruit, some were pulling wagons loaded with sacks and buckets, or driving a goat or a fat pig with a stick. A man in his fifties passed with a carriage pulled by a donkey. "Slow, slow, brrrrrr…" he said, bringing the donkey to a halt.

"Look what pots and cauldrons I'm carrying," he said to me. "If you want the best choice, this is your chance, friend. Take a good look, the maiden too, please."

We didn't show much interest in his products.

"You off to market?" he asked, with a broad smile showing gaps in his teeth.

"Oh, it's market day today?" I asked in reply.

"Of course. What a question. Why else do you think all these traders are heading to Hamberton? Best day of the week—at least for us sellers!" he said, laughing. "So do you want to take a closer look?"

But as we thanked him and shook our heads, he whacked the donkey with his stick to trot on, to the market where there would be lots of other customers! That would be the right place to find out all we needed to know. We followed the man through the entrance to the town, and round the corner. After passing rows of small thatched houses and gardens, we ended up in an open square filled with people and stalls. The sellers were unpacking their wares from large wicker baskets, wooden boxes and small hand wagons, already offering what they had to sell. Each one praised their own goods, trying to catch the attention of potential buyers: "The finest and sweetest apples from all of Mercia, you won't get any better than here!" or "Cheese, cheese, best cheese from well-fed cows," or "Pots and pans, pots and pans, roll up for pots and pans!"

Soon the market place was packed. There was a constant stream of people coming and going, stopping here and there to chat or to haggle over what they wanted to buy. The ground was dusty, and in the breeze it swirled up and stuck to hands and foreheads. At a stall with wooden buckets, a heavy man with a beige tunica, his sleeves rolled up, plunged a hand into the bucket and pulled out a grey fish which he offered us. The fishy scent assaulted our noses as we walked passed, shaking our heads with a tired smile. A little old woman sat on a stool with bunches of spicy-smelling herbs spread out on the ground in front of her. She had constructed a small roof behind her with four sticks holding a piece of cloth that provided a small patch of shade. We stopped—she wasn't crying out her bargains, and we needed a break. The noise, the dust, the heat were tiring.

The old lady's little eyes glinted from a sea of wrinkles as she spotted us.

"My dearies, how can I help you?" she croaked. "Do you have a headache or problems with your stomach? Are you not getting enough sleep, or not getting pregnant?" She picked up one of the sprigs of herbs, as if she already had the cure for whatever problem we might have.

"Oh, no no," Rohanna answered, declining her offer.

"You are looking a little worried, my dearie," the old lady said, her hand sheltering her eyes from the dazzling sun.

The shouting of the shoppers and the leather-shod footsteps crunching on the gravel caused a constant background noise. I bent down to the old lady so that I wouldn't have to raise my voice.

"Thank you! We are quite well," I said. "But maybe you could help us with something else…"

"Oh, sure. Go ahead!" the old lady said, smiling and nodding.

Rohanna knelt down too, so that the woman wouldn't have to shelter her eyes from the sun when looking up.

"Do you know a monastery near Hamberton?"

"The friary of St Martin's? That's the one closest to here," the old lady answered.

"Is it only a short walk from here—or is there another monastery nearby?"

"There's only St Martin's—it's the only one around here. There are others, mind you, but they're at least a day's walk away," she said, shaking a hand in the air, chasing away flies. "Are you not from here? I have a son in the friary and a nephew, bless them. Do you need to go there?"

"Yes, we'd like to visit the friary. We've been there before, you see … well, it was quite a while ago!" I said with a meaningful glance to Rohanna, who nodded in confirmation.

"I can't remember seeing you around these parts before," the old lady said. "And believe me, I've been around for a very long time!" she chuckled.

Despite the stuffy heat, I felt a cold wave rush through my heart. What if we had arrived at the wrong time after all? I didn't dare to look at Rohanna.

"So you want to know how to get there?" the old lady asked.

"Yes," Rohanna answered, nodding eagerly.

Then it slipped out of my mouth: "Is Father Bede still at the friary?" I held my breath.

"Oh, Father Bede, bless him…" the old lady said. But before she could continue, another elderly woman interrupted her.

"Hildreth, let me have some of your mint," she said, pointing at the herbs. "Mine hasn't grown well and I really need this mint. I miss it and you've got plenty. So how much, love, for that bushel?"

"Oh, yours didn't grow this year? I hope that doesn't mean bad luck!"

"Ah, nonsense," the other woman answered. "I'm not superstitious. Oh, and by the way, give me some sage too, I could do with a little more. I'll be drying the leaves and will need them for treating teeth. It's always good to have enough in stock."

"What about something for the friary?" the market woman said. "Aren't you going there soon? You could take these young souls down there," she added, and placed a bunch of garlic into the buyer's hand.

"Oh, could you point us the direction?" I asked. We knew the monastery wasn't far, but we had never travelled from Hamberton before.

"My friend will show you the way there, won't you, honey?" the old lady asked.

The other woman paid a few coins for her wares and tucked the herbs in a bag that hung around her shoulders. Soon we were following her through the market.

"Have you got relatives in the monastery?" she asked as she marched ahead, waving now and then to passers-by and exchanging greetings or a few words.

"No, we don't have relatives, but we are friends with the monks," I answered, while I truly hoped that those friends were still around.

When we came to the end of the market, the bustle and hustle petered out; the path led along some quiet huts and gardens and small meadows, with goats running up to us as we passed by. We reached the end of the town and were out in the countryside. A sea of heather stretched ahead as we took the path towards the edge of the forest. The scent from the purple flowers filled the air, as well as the sound of buzzing bees.

On the hills we could see smaller settlements, and after ten minutes the path split in two. "I'm going up this path," the elderly woman said, pointing towards a hill that bore one of the small settlements. "But you folks need to carry on down here to get to the friary. Just skirt the heather, following the edge of the forest. You'll go round the corner and then downhill, after which you'll soon see the monastery wall. When you arrive there, give the monks my blessings!"

"Who shall we mention?" I asked.

"Oh, just tell them, from his cousin."

"Whose cousin?"
"I'm Bede's cousin, see!" And with that she left.

Chapter Twenty—Back at the Friary

I stopped in my tracks. It was quiet apart from the buzzing of bees and the occasional tweet from the forest.

"She said she's a cousin of Bede!" I cried. "That must mean he's still alive!"

"Are you sure?" Rohanna asked. "Saying that she's his cousin doesn't have to mean he's still alive…"

"I'm sure it was meant that he's still there…" I answered. "Otherwise she would've had to say: 'I'm a cousin of Bede who used to be the prior of the monastery,' or something like that."

"Well, I hope so," Rohanna answered. "It would be some good news!"

"Bede was around forty years old (at least, he was when *we* saw him last)," I began calculating. A cousin is often a similar age—but this woman looked quite old."

"You're right," Rohanna sighed. "She must've been in her early seventies, and that would mean Bede could already be—over sixty or seventy years old!"

"But what if she's just a much older cousin?" I asked.

"What if she's a younger one?" Rohanna added.

"Oh, let's just stop. We'll soon find out anyway once we get there," I said.

We walked on for about ten minutes. The smell of heather in the air mingled with the smell of moss and leaves as the path skirted the forest edge. Several people passed us on their way to Hamberton or another village, and greeted us with a nod. We hardly talked until we discovered the grey wall of the monastery. My heart beat as we approached its gate. It looked hardly different from those many years ago. At the porch stood a monk, whom I didn't recognise. That doesn't have to mean anything, I told myself. After all, there were around a dozen or so monks, and I never got to know them all. They probably swapped duties, so that now another monk was guarding the porch rather than the one it had been last time I was here.

The monk had slightly reddish hair and a short beard. He might have been around thirty years old.

We stood still in front of the entrance. "Hail, who do you wish to see?" the porter asked.

Rohanna looked at me. We hadn't thought of what to say. Should we ask to see Bede? But what if he wasn't still alive?

"Could we see Bede?" I asked, while my heart stood still.

"Are you friends of Bede?" the porter asked.

"Yes, we're old friends," I answered, full of hope. "Is he here? Are we allowed to see him?"

"I will bring you to the guest room," the porter answered, beckoning us to follow.

We entered the monastery garden, and walked past the circular vegetable and herb beds, past the berry bushes with the sweet smell of raspberries. The sun shone down warm, but the monastery walls provided some shade, keeping the garden cooler than on the open path. I sweated as my heartbeat increased. We were now minutes or seconds away from the truth. We passed the chapel and reached the entrance to the long stone building. The monk pushed the bolt aside and led us into the corridor and into the first room on the right.

"Please, wait here," he said. "Father Bede will come soon."

We each took a seat on the chairs placed around a table with a small vase of flowers on it. I remembered staring at the same stone walls when I had come here for the first time as a twelve-year-old. The little square window showed the same view out to the distant hills and forests and the leaves dancing in the summer air. It was very quiet, as if no one lived here. The minutes waiting felt like hours, and for a moment I wondered if the porter had forgotten us. It was pleasantly cool with the breeze blowing through the open window. The atmosphere would have made me sleepy, if I hadn't been so tense.

Rohanna held one hand in the other, wringing her fingers and pressing her lips. Then we heard footsteps approaching and we both shot up. Just a moment later, Bede stood in the doorway.

"Father Bede!" I exclaimed at his appearance. Rohanna and I almost hugged him. I examined his face. His hair was still dark brown, but with single grey hairs. His eyes had the same wise and moderate expression as he smiled on seeing us. He was much the same as I had left him, with a few more wrinkles on his face.

"So you're back!" he said nodding. "I *thought* it wouldn't take long for you to find your way back! Or perhaps I should say, to be *brought* back... You have grown, Adrian!"

"Oh, I'm so glad *you're* here," I said, and I really meant it. But it probably sounded strange.

Brother Bede raised his eyebrows and asked: "Well, where else would I be?"

"Of course, nowhere else than here in the monastery... But, you see, on our side, a long time has passed, much more than in your world, and I don't take it for granted that you are still here!" I added.

Bede raised his eyebrows. "Is this your sister?" he asked, examining us both.

"Yes, she's Rohanna." I introduced my twin sister.

"I'm pleased to meet you," Bede said, shaking her hand. "Have you already been to the village?" he asked. He didn't need to explain which village, we all knew he meant Durwyn's village.

Rohanna shook her head with a nervous smile. She must have been glad—Father Bede was present after all, and he hadn't even turned into an old man yet! And this meant the chances were high that Durwyn and the rest were also still around.

"No, we haven't been to the village yet," I told him. "We've just been to Hamberton market, but we had a long journey getting here. It began in the Norse country—well actually before." Then I poured out everything about our Norse friends who wanted to live in Mercia instead of joining raids with the other Vikings, the journey across the sea, the monsters and the near death experiences, the Picts and our encounter with the monks in Wales. All the while he listened thoughtfully.

"Bring your friends to the village," Bede said at the end of my narrative. "The villagers there have good hearts and will help the Norse to begin a new life here in Mercia."

"Yes, that's what we intended to do. I'm glad you're supporting us with that idea," I said. Then Bede stroked his chin and narrowed his eyebrows. "You mentioned that there might be other Vikings coming to Mercia."

"Yes, and not all are as peaceful as these. They are planning a raid on Mercia, but I don't know when exactly," I answered.

Bede nodded and said: "I have heard of raids in other parts of the country. And these kinds of Vikings often target monasteries."

"Why monasteries?" Rohanna asked.

"They expect to find precious treasures in monasteries. And they do—for example golden chalices and metal crosses in churches. But it's also because monks are unarmed. We don't train for killing, we train for saving souls."

"Well, I hope they never come this far inland, and your monastery stays unharmed," I said.

Bede fell silent until he suddenly asked: "What is your plan now?"

"We need to go to Durwyn's village," I said, looking at Rohanna. "As you said, we will bring the Norse to the village and perhaps we can all settle down there."

I didn't dare mention that Rohanna would want to meet Durwyn. I didn't know how much Bede knew about them both. Most importantly, Bede was alive and had hardly changed. Not many years could have passed here in Mercia.

Suddenly, I thought of a question which would clarify this. I hadn't thought of it before, but most people of Mercia probably wouldn't have been able to answer the question, whereas the monks were literate and educated. And so I asked: "Do you know what year it is now?"

"Well, of course," he said. "It's anno domini (which means the year of God) seven hundred and ninety-five."

"795," I repeated. Rohanna looked puzzled.

"We'd also have to know what year..." Rohanna began.

"Can you tell me what year it was when we were here last time?" I hastily completed her question.

Bede pulled his eyebrows together, "When was it? Five summers ago? It must have been ... yes, it must have been anno domini 790."

"Five years ago!" I exclaimed. Rohanna turned pale.

"We'll be going now," I said. I didn't know if Bede knew anything about Durwyn and Rohanna. I didn't want Bede to say anything before she had seen Durwyn herself. Anything could have happened within five years. Anything... But now, at least we knew that he could still be around, and if so, certainly was still young. I just hoped he'd be alive. Didn't he sometimes accompany his father to war? But if he was alive and well, the most important question still remained: Five years had gone by—had he been waiting for Rohanna all that time?

When we left the monastery, it was around three in the afternoon according to the position of the sun. The air had heated up like an oven and shimmered above the path, as it does on hot days like this. We stopped at a stream to cool our foreheads and to drink. Rohanna combed her hair and tied it up again. She bit her lips and I saw she was both worried and full of anticipation. What if ... what if ... seemed to be written across her face.

"Don't worry," I tried to calm her. "Just don't worry. The worst that could have happened to him would be him being dead. You can't change things, anyway..."

"Oh, thank you," she said sarcastically. But then she shook her head: "No, the worst would be if he'd been given away," she said, biting her lips again. I was surprised how openly we talked about it. Perhaps the heat loosened us up.

"Do you think he would've agreed to that?" I asked.

"Half of me says no—he must have waited. But the other half says, I'm just so naïve and our reunion is never going to happen."

"You've got to be prepared for both. But if he's taken ... you needn't worry! There'll be enough men around who will ask for your hand instead. And you'd be free and unbound to agree to any one of them!"

"Oh, let's just stop," she said sighing.

"It's not far now," I announced as the path came to a turning point. In front of us slopes of green hills scattered with settlements and partly covered with patches of forest. "There," I said pointing ahead. "That's Durwyn's village, and I can see the hill with the chapel behind it!" Rohanna shielded her eyes from the sun and nodded in agreement. My heart started to beat louder. "It will take us around twenty minutes," I guessed. Twenty minutes until we would reach the gate of Durwyn's village...

Chapter Twenty-One—Back at the Village

The wooden gate framed with colourful carved swirls looked the same as years ago. It was late in the afternoon, and due to the heat there was hardly anyone outside. A young woman came out of a hut to draw water, but vanished back inside without seeing us; an elderly man sat under an apple tree, and the sheep and cows were out in the meadow gathered under the shade of trees. The corn in the fields was ripening, and poppies and cornflowers grew along the fields' edge, spreading a sweet scent to attract the bees. Apart from an occasional cackle of a hen and the buzzing of bees the village was quiet, dreaming along through the hot summer's day.

What should we do next? Knock on the door where Durwyn used to live, or sit down and wait for the villagers to discover us? We were tired from the walk and the heat made it hard to think clearly. So in the end we sat down on a big stone in the shade of a walnut tree, near the fence with its pointed tips. From here we could watch over the village. From here we recognised Durwyn's home, or at least where he used to live. The hut stood 20 metres away from us, partly hidden by other huts that stood in front of it, but we could make out the entrance.

I offered Rohanna the rest of water that was left in the skin bottle. She took a sip or two, but she was neither thirsty nor hungry. Not knowing what was going to happen next weighed upon her. Would she soon be relieved of that weight, or would it crush her?

Then the door of Durwyn's hut opened and a girl of about six years of age hopped out. Her hair was golden brown and tied back in a ponytail. She ran to another hut, without noticing the strangers sitting on the stone. She banged on the door and shouted something which I couldn't make out. The other hut stood a little further up the hill, at the back of the village, close to the fence. Branches of an oak tree hung over the fence, casting shade on the hut.

The little girl carried a basket. When the door opened, a young man stood in the porch. He was wearing a brown apron and looked as if he had been working. His hair was gold-blond, like the girl's but slightly darker, and it fell in waves on his shoulders. He had a roundish face, but from where we sat, we couldn't see clearly. His tunica sleeves were rolled up, revealing muscular arms. He wasn't very tall and his wide chest suggested that he was used to physical work. He brushed some strands of hair back and took a bundle from the girl. They exchanged a few words before the girl turned around and skipped back to where she had come from. Halfway there she stopped and stared curiously down to the rock where we were sitting.

"This could be Fridogitha!" I whispered excitedly. "And couldn't that be … Durwyn who opened the door?"

"I thought so too…" Rohanna answered, holding on to my arm. "The girl won't recognise us, though. She was too small to remember … and if it is him," (and by "him" she of course meant Durwyn) "that would mean he is now living in another house."

"Wasn't that the house he had begun to build with his father? Remember, he showed us shortly before we went back to our world."

"Yes, I remember the planks that were lying ready for the building. That must be it now…" Rohanna said, tightening the grip on my arm. "But what if he's sharing his house with someone else already?"

"It doesn't have to be!" I tried to calm her. But how could I know? Perhaps she was right. Perhaps Durwyn was married and had his own family now and we would appear as intruders. I tried to hide that terrifying thought, I didn't want to weigh Rohanna down even more.

After observing us briefly, the girl skipped on back to her home. Was she going to tell her parents that there were strangers outside? People would probably leave their huts towards evening, when the sun is lower and it was less hot. We still had the option just to silently leave. We could go back to our Viking friends and start a new life somewhere else, together with them.

But before we made up our minds what to do next, the door opened again and out came a middle-aged woman together with the girl. And they both headed straight towards us.

Chapter Twenty-Two—Reunion

Rohanna and I stood up. As soon as the girl and the woman were closer, we recognised it was Goda—the mother of Fridogitha and Durwyn!

"Is it *you*?" she asked as soon as she was near enough. "Is it really you?" A broad smile crossed her face and she opened her arms to embrace us. "You have grown! And look how you've both turned handsome and pretty! Durwyn is going to be happy to see you," she said, gripping Rohanna's arm.

"When did you arrive?"

"Just a few minutes ago," Rohanna answered.

"You must be thirsty in this heat! Come along to the hut," she said, and led us into her home.

"Fridogitha, look, these are Durwyn's friends—you probably don't remember them," Goda said to her daughter.

The girl shook her head, but smiled broadly, which made her look like her mother. "I can't remember myself, but I do remember hearing a lot about you!"

During our first visit to Mercia, Fridogitha had been much smaller and didn't talk yet. Seeing her now, I remembered how she was miraculously healed of the dark fever, after we had returned the leech book and when Halig had mixed up the medicine. She had changed a lot—her face was less chubby and she had grown into the size of a girl who, in our world, would be attending school.

Goda hadn't changed much—perhaps there were a few more wrinkles on her face and a couple of grey hairs mixed in her brown hair. Her skin had a golden-brown colour from working outside.

"In this hot weather you need refreshment. Some peppermint water will do the job."

Although we had been sitting in the shade before, the air had been so hot it had made us sweaty and sticky. Stepping into the cool hut was like entering an oasis. There were no windows and now I realised how convenient that was, keeping out the sunlight and heat.

Everything looked the same as it had before. There was currently no fire burning, but like last time there were sprigs of drying herbs hung from the ceiling, the beds lining the wall were covered with pelts, and the air was filled with the smell of herbs, wood and leather.

Goda poured water from a jug standing in a dark corner of the hut into two mugs. I eagerly drank the cool, minty water. I hadn't noticed how thirsty I was from walking in the heat.

"I will tell Durwyn to come over," Goda said, patting Rohanna's hand as if she could read her thoughts. "He's got his own home all set up now. But he's still working on the inside. He's doing a lot of carving these days, when he finds time between field work and taking care of the cattle," she said. "He's been thinking of you a lot, I believe," she added with a twinkle in her eye.

Rohanna looked at me but didn't dare to comment. What could she say? This was probably the most important moment of her life—she had been waiting so long for this to happen. In my mind, I began to work things out: As we had learned from Bede, five years had passed since we had been here. But for us, we were actually returning after many decades, although we hadn't turned old. Perhaps we were now precisely that five years older since last time! The first time we had come to Mercia, we were twelve and a half. In that case, we must now be seventeen and a half…

"Come with me," Goda said to Fridogitha. "Let's go and ask Durwyn to come over, but without telling him who's here. We'll just say there's a surprise."

Goda and Fridogitha went out and we watched them through the open door as they approached his hut and knocked on the door.

"Come on in," his voice sounded from the inside.

"You need to come out!" Goda said.

"All right, all right… have the cattle run off again?"

"Not at all," said his mother.

Instead of bringing him to her hut, she led him to a bench that stood in the shade of the beech trees near the fence. She told him to wait there.

"He's out there waiting; you'd better go now," she said to Rohanna when she returned to us.

Rohanna stood up, flattened the creases in her dress again and gave me one more look with raised eyebrows.

"Good luck," I said, smiling.

She smiled back, her lips pressed tightly together.

I stood at the entrance and watched as she neared the little bench where Durwyn sat. As soon as she was close enough to be recognised, Durwyn stood up. The surprise was written all over his body. And then it was just the two of them. They just stood there for a few seconds glancing at each other before Durwyn took her hand and sat down with her on the bench; and nobody knew, apart from them, what words were exchanged—if any at all—and how they looked in each other's eyes and what they felt. I saw my sister finally united with the one she had waited for, and I knew one chapter had come to an end and a new one—of them both together—had just begun.

"Durwyn's been waiting all these years for your sister," Goda said. "He didn't want anyone else, even when there were several opportunities! I'm glad she's returned. It's a blessing!"

"Yes," I said, "it *is* a blessing," and I meant it truly. "She's been waiting for him too…" I added. I didn't mention how long it had been for her, though. What did it matter, anyway? It seemed that love doesn't have a time limit, doesn't distinguish between countries, and not even between worlds!

The time had come when I had to let go of Rohanna and leave her with Durwyn. I was happy for them both and wished them all the best fortune (thank God, everything had gone well). But I also suddenly felt a void in me. I thought of my own wife, Veronica, whom I had lost years ago. And even though I wouldn't have admitted it to anyone, I felt alone in this world. Rohanna had reached her destination. But what about me? What was my goal here in Mercia? I couldn't imagine marrying again. I had been married once and there was no repeat for me. I wouldn't have wanted to replace Veronica. You could call me stubborn, the same stubbornness that Rohanna had and which made her wait for Durwyn for decades. She didn't take another man, and I wouldn't replace my late wife.

"Do you think Durwyn's going to marry now?" Fridogitha asked, skipping around her mother.

"Oh, I'm quite certain about that," she answered. "But first they'll need to talk to the priest."

"Yes!" Fridogitha exclaimed and threw her arms up in the air and clapped her hands. "I can't wait for a wedding to happen! The last one I went to was my cousin's. But that was already two summers ago. I'll want to gather flowers for the bride's hair and dress, and pretty myself."

"Patience, my little girl! Now go back to cooking. It'll soon be evening and I need the fire burning."

Fridogitha kneeled down by the fire and placed small sticks carefully in a circle. She kindled the fire and Goda brought a cauldron to put on the flames. Then they both began cutting vegetables.

I realised that Goda not only had more creases around her mouth from smiling, but also more creases on her forehead as if from worrying. As she chopped the vegetables, it looked as if something sad crossed her mind, and I wondered where Durwyn's father was.

"How is Durwyn's father?" I asked. There was a short silence as Goda interrupted her work. I knew that something had happened to him. Perhaps I was too direct with my question and I shouldn't ask more. But Goda sighed. "My husband, Ealdian," she said, "he was fighting in a battle ... and didn't make it back home."

"I'm sorry," I said cautiously, feeling a lump in my throat. She shook her head and carried on cutting carrots, while Fridogitha threw sliced leeks into the cauldron and added a thick dab of butter. The butter sizzled as it melted and a delicious smell of fried leek filled the air.

"He was a brave fighter—God bless his soul," she continued. I nodded, lost for words.

I looked at Fridogitha and wondered if she remembered her father. I could still see how he had lifted her high onto his shoulders, out of joy over her recovery, when we returned the leech book. He had carried her round the village shouting out his victory at battle and over her illness. He had been an example to me. He knew how to fight in real battles with sword and shield; he knew how to plough the fields and milk the cows. And now he was gone.

"How do you manage all the farm work?" I asked Goda, knowing that there was so much to do, more than one grown-up could do on her own.

"Durwyn is here to help and does the work my husband used to: feeding and caring for the cattle and so on. But we villagers also help each other out all the time. I'm not alone," she said, but there was something heavy in her voice. She was still suffering from the loss, but nevertheless wanted to appear strong. Maybe it was for the sake of Fridogitha. The young girl seemed happy and carefree.

"Do you remember your father?" I dared to ask her.

"A little bit," she said, while swaying her head to and fro. "Not much really, just a little bit."

I wanted to tell Goda about the loss *I* had experienced, but hesitated. How could she understand? Why would she believe that in the other world I had already been much older? And so I kept it to myself.

"We have Norse friends waiting for us on a hill near Hamberton," I said to change the subject. "They are camping there, as they would like to begin a new life here in Mercia."

"You have friends from the land of the Norse?" she asked, surprised. I remembered that the Norse were from the same country as the men who must have killed her husband. I lowered my head, but I couldn't take back my words. "Yes, they're from the Norse country," I said cautiously. "But don't worry, they aren't coming to raid or cause havoc... They are peaceful and all they want is to settle down and farm the land."

"If they're your friends, they're always welcome to start living here," she said. "How many are there?"

"There's Bard and his wife," I began, counting on my fingers. "Ragnar, an elderly man, then Astrid and Ljot who have two little children; there's Karl, and Bard's two grown-up sons Erik and Bjorn. It's ten in all—without Rohanna and me."

"I will talk to the other villagers. Our men can help them build their huts. Summer's a good time for building, before the weather turns cold again. Where is the camp—what shelter have they found?"

I told her about the place on the hill near the wood, how we had built a temporary shelter. Now I'd be able to bring them some good news!

"We'll go back to the camp this evening and tell them about your village. They'll be delighted to hear that they're welcome to settle down here. They are still recovering from the journey, but in one or two days I will return with them."

"There's not much food left in the camp," I began worrying. But before I could ask her to help us out, she got up and said: "I will give you food to take along with you. My neighbour has been baking bread today, and someone else can give you pork and lamb which they have plentifully."

It would soon be evening and we had promised to be back before nightfall. I stepped out of Goda's hut and waved to Rohanna and Durwyn. They shot up from the bench and came to the hut smiling all over. Durwyn and I met and shook hands, laughing. He hadn't changed much in these five years, although he seemed more mature, and there was something more sincere and melancholic in his eyes than before.

"So, has it been worth the wait?" I asked, grinning.

"Absolutely," Durwyn said, putting his arm round Rohanna's shoulder, as if to say he'd never separate from her again. Rohanna beamed and I knew she was the happiest ever.

"Did you tell him about our Norse friends at the camp?" I asked Rohanna. "I think it would be good to go back now and let them know how things stand."

"Yes, I've told him and he offered to come along with us," she answered.

"You know, it will be a good thing for our village to expand," he said. "I'm looking forward to meeting your Norse friends. I will also help them build houses, and so will the other villagers."

Soon Goda was back with sacks of food. Durwyn got ready for the walk to the camp—and we left Goda and Fridogitha, promising to be back in about two days.

The way back was quicker, as we didn't stop at the monastery and didn't pass through Hamberton. By the time we reached the foot of the hill, where the camp was, it was starting to get dark. I discovered the track where we had been walking earlier, but there were also animal tracks.

This was going to be difficult, since there was no proper path and the wood looked everywhere the same. How would we find the shelter before dark? Then Durwyn pointed further uphill. There was smoke coming from a place a short way from where we stood.

"Could this be where your camp is?" he asked, watching the grey pillar of smoke rise to the sky.

"Yes! That must be it! We're lucky that they're cooking right now!"

"Perhaps they aren't cooking," Durwyn said.

"What do you mean?" I asked.

"Making a fire is a good way to signal where you are in the wilderness! All you then have to do is follow the smoke…"

Chapter Twenty-Three—Revealing the Call

It didn't take long for us to reach the camp, where there were now two shelters—they had built a second one while we were away. The hearth lay between the two shelters, and Helga and Astrid were busy roasting meat over the embers.

Bard saw us approaching: "Ha! Our friends! I knew you wouldn't let us down. It was getting boring here. I can't wait to get to work. Now, I'm curious to know what news you bring us!"

We introduced him and the others to Durwyn. Our Norse friends had been working on their English phrases in the meantime and were now using them proudly. They soon became friends with Durwyn and engaged in a funny kind of discussion. Erik, Bjorn and Karl showed him with hand gesticulations and single words in English and the rest in Norse how they had constructed the shelters. Durwyn taught them missing words in English, which they were eager to learn.

During our walk back to the camp, something was on my mind. Even though I spoke to Rohanna and Durwyn, I was focused on other thoughts. An idea had come to me which I had never had before. When Rohanna and Durwyn were reunited, it was as if I was giving away Rohanna, my close sister, and I became aware of a certain loneliness. But now I felt a strong urge to take on a new path in my life. The idea for this might have been sparked in Wales, when we were hosted by the ascetic monks for some hours. I was attracted to their way of life, but didn't think of living like that myself.

But after returning to Hamberton monastery with Father Bede and the monks still there, monastery life had become familiar to me. Now, while walking back to the camp, I suddenly had the idea to … yes, to become a monk myself! What a comforting idea, to leave the world behind! Members of a monastery chose not to marry or be in a close relationship with anyone other than with God. If I became a monk, I would find a new purpose in life. I'd learn to garden, make handicrafts, bake, and write books with a feather and ink and illuminate the initial letters with beautiful colourful ornamentation. I'd wake up early and go early to bed. I'd get up at night for prayer in the chapel, then go back to sleep for a few hours. I'd help and feed the poor and teach others to read and write.

This idea filled me with joy: it was a new kind of joy, like discovering a new land you didn't even know existed before, and I wondered why I hadn't thought of the idea before. In modern England, a monastic life seemed something solely of the past. Hardly anything was left behind of that past, apart from ruins of former monasteries and churches, scattered across the country. Now and then one would hear a legend about a British saint. But here in Mercia it was different. Monastic life was something people were used to.

I decided not to tell anyone yet about me becoming a monk. First I wanted to talk to Bede about it. He was the leader of the Hamberton friary, so he'd be the one I'd ask for permission to join. I wondered: Would the monks find me worthy of entering their monastery? Why not? I asked myself. I had once been married, but now I was a widower. Nothing stood in my way. I now so strongly desired to enter the monastery, I couldn't imagine anything else. I had to talk to Bede as soon as possible!

That night, everyone had enough space to spread out because there were now two shelters. At night I kept thinking of the monastery. I was glad that Erik, Bjorn and Karl hadn't been very talkative that evening. In fact they were unusually quiet, as if they had something on their mind, too. But I didn't have time to think of that. Tomorrow I would visit the monastery on my own and speak to Bede. I was ready to enter monastic life right away, and hoped I wouldn't have to wait. There was nothing else I wanted more than to live as a monk! That night I began to focus on God. I thought about He who had created me, the land, the earth and the whole universe. Life was strange and yet beautiful, I thought, before drifting off to sleep.

Next morning Durwyn was going to bring us to the village. I planned to walk with the others until shortly before Hamberton, then I would tell them that I needed to talk to Bede and separate from the group. Well, at least, that's what I *planned* to do.

But then I happened to sit by the fire with Bjorn, Karl and Erik while the others were busy mending clothes, looking for berries and mushrooms or playing with Olfi and the baby. I knew the three had something on their mind, because they were quieter than usual.

Erik picked up a damp stick, broke it in half and threw the bits in the fire. We watched as it popped and crackled as the dew came into contact with the flames.

"Ye know," Erik began with a sigh, "I don't think we —that's Karl, Bjorn and I—are going to live in the Anglo-Saxon village, after all!"

"What?" I asked, surprised. "Do you want to go back to Norse land, after all we've been through?"

"Nay, I didn't say we're going back. I just said we don't want to live in yer village…"

"Well, it's not really *my* village," I said. "It's Durwyn's village … but I admit, it's the place in Mercia that Rohanna and I are most familiar with."

"Whatever. It's not about this village or in fact any village," Erik carried on. "I've made up me mind. I wish to go back to that monks' place in Cymry and start that way of living."

"You want to live as a monk?" I asked, staring at him.

"Yes—and it's not just me…" Erik dug with another stick in the glowing ashes. "To be honest, earlier on, we three all hoped that we'd either take your sister Rohanna for a wife, or each find another woman among the Angles and Saxons. That was the plan, weren't it?" he asked the others. They nodded in agreement.

"So, why do you give up so soon? Even if Rohanna's taken, there're plenty of other women."

"Oh, man. It's not about the women. Don't ye think we could easily get a wife? Course we could—or at least I could," he said, chuckling. "Nay, I've noticed, there's more to life than eat, sleep, work, fight. And I always kind of knew it, but only after being with the monks have I come to understand," he said.

"What about Karl and Bjorn? Have you told them to follow you?" I asked.

"Ha, follow me? As if it would be that easy… They wouldn't listen to me, would they? I didn't tell 'em what I was thinking. But yesterday evening, there comes Erik and he says: 'I'm gonna live like them monks. I've had this dream, and not just 'cause of it.' Ye see, he's convinced, like me."

"And you, Karl?" I asked.

Karl nodded, glancing thoughtfully at the glowing embers. "It's the same for me. I hear an inner voice that's telling me to go and live as a monk. I want to learn more of what I've seen there in Cymry. Yeu must think we've gone berserk, but nay. It's what I *want*—and I won't get me peace unless I can go back to them monks."

"Well," I began, "let me tell you this: there's also a monastery nearby—next to Hamberton—and I know the monks there." I took a short breath. "And because I've lost my wife earlier (it's a long story), I myself have…"

"Decided to become a monk?" Erik asked.

"You name it."

"Heavens," Bjorn said, "it was already quite something if us three become monks. But now *ye* too?" They chuckled.

"Are ye serious?" Karl asked, while redoing his black plait.

I nodded. "Yes, I mean it."

"Ye never told us ye were married before," Bjorn said, staring at me. "Don't ye want to get a new wife?"

I shook my head. "I don't think I could replace Veronica," I said, surprised by my own certainty. "I can show you the monastery nearby. Perhaps you will like it too."

"We can 'ave a look, and after that decide which monastery to go to," Erik said.

"But there is a problem," Bjorn said, sighing. "Our parents… They won't be pleased with our decision. I mean, not wanting to marry, not possessing a house … don't it sound mad?"

"Just tell them there's something you want more than that…"

"They 'ave other plans in mind for us. They want us to build houses, 'ave a family, work the fields…"

"We'll help 'em build their house, of course," Bjorn said. "But at some point, we're gonna have to open up. And it's not gonna be easy!"

"It may help if we all just go to talk with Father Bede," I said.

"Is that yer father?" Karl asked.

"No, no. He's the leading monk in the Hamberton monastery," I said. "They call him father, because he's like a father to the monks."

Before we left, I had a chance to talk to Rohanna on her own. "Erik, Bjorn, Karl and I are going to Hamberton monastery to discuss something," I said, trying to sound casual.

"What for?" she asked. I wasn't ready to tell her about my ambitions. "I just want to talk about a few things concerning life. Father Bede's a good listener and a good leader at the same time."

"I know you're up to something…" she said. It was hard to hide anything from Rohanna. She knew me too well.

"Listen," I told her. "You take over translating, while I'm at the monastery. The Norse and the villagers need to get to know each other without hostile feelings. Your translating will help the two peoples learn to understand each other and get along. The Norse friends have to feel welcome. They need a new home…"

Rohanna agreed, and it was only when I spoke those words that we became aware of how important this was. If the Norse weren't welcomed, where could they go and how could they settle down?

Durwyn, Bard and Ragnar led the group along our track downhill, which was still visible from walking up the hill before. Astrid had the baby in a sling and Helga walked with Rohanna, asking her questions about the new place they'd be living in, while Ljot carried Olfi on his shoulders. When we were some distance away from the camp, I looked back to check if our shelters were visible. I could recognise the two green roofs of the shelters and signs of the fire, but they were hardly visible as they mingled with the nature around—a camouflage dwelling.

Chapter Twenty-Four—Talk with Bede

We were quite close to the gate of the monastery when I tugged Erik, Bjorn and Karl and pulled them over to me. "This is where we need to go now," I whispered and pointed to the gates of the monastery. As we then skirted the forest edge, I said to Bard: "Erik, Bjorn, Karl and I are going to separate from the group here. Just carry on, we'll follow up later…"

He looked at me, surprised. "But we're not at the village yet, ain't we?"

"No, no. Keep following Durwyn. Rohanna will help with translating."

He stood still. "What is this place?" he asked, looking at the gate under the stony arch.

"It's … oh, I have some old friends here whom I need to introduce to Karl, Bjorn and Erik. We will catch up soon, I promise."

"Why do ye 'ave to go there now?"

"I'll explain later," I said, ushering the other three towards the gate.

Then I waved goodbye as Bard carried on down the path with the group.

It was late afternoon, and the monks were gathered in the chapel for early evening prayers. We slipped into the chapel and took a seat on a bench at the back. The stone walls of the chapel resonated with the low and medium voices of the singing monks. We sat there listening for a quiet while. I couldn't tell how much time passed: was it ten minutes or half an hour? The chanting lifted my soul as the melody moved back and forth, like gentle waves. The others sat quietly listening and looking up to the chapel's ceiling, and sometimes down, with their hands over their face, as if looking deep into their soul. This singing could have gone on for ever, what did it matter? In this heavenly state, time lost its meaning. The monks stood up after a certain phrase in the chant, and then, still singing, they walked past us along the aisle. If they were surprised when they discovered our presence, they didn't show it. We followed them outside while they carried on singing, before each vanished into a cell in the long building.

"Now what?" Erik asked. "How will we get to talk to them?"

"Don't worry," I answered. I led them to the small room where I used to wait during the other times when visiting the monastery. "They have seen us, and sooner or later one of them will come here." We waited for a few minutes, and then I heard the familiar soft padding of feet and Father Bede appeared at the open door, his arms tucked in his sleeves and his brown eyes examining each of us briefly.

"Adrian," he began, "it is good to see you." Father Bede sounded as if he'd been expecting me.

"Are these the Norse men you've been talking about?" he asked, looking at Erik, Bjorn and Karl.

"Yes," I answered. "Erik and Bjorn are brothers and Karl is their neighbour. They've grown up in the same village in Norseland."

Bede nodded.

"So now it is your intention to settle in Durwyn's village?" he asked them.

"Yes, their family and friends certainly do," I answered for them.

"Good, good," Father Bede said, and raised his hand over their heads. "May God bless you and lead you to a new life here in Mercia. Is there anything I can do for you?" he asked.

I took a deep breath. "Do you have time to talk?" I asked, almost not daring to take more of his time. The monks had a daily routine, and everything had a purpose. Perhaps Bede didn't have time to talk with us about our personal concerns.

"Wait," he said and then left the room. Before long he returned with another monk, both carrying chairs for us. The other monk left again without a word.

"Father Bede," I began, "you know that I come from another world, or let's say another time." Father Bede nodded. As Erik, Bjorn and Karl didn't yet understand everything, I dared to disclose more.

"I was married there, but my wife died long ago," I continued. "I was already old, back in the other world, and now, can you believe it? Here in Mercia, I am young again!" Father Bede glanced at me for a short moment and nodded again. Was he impressed or not? I couldn't tell. If he was, he wasn't showing it.

"I can't explain how all this happened…" I said and paused.

Father Bede said: "Sometimes we're unable to understand God's ways. We just have to accept how things are and perhaps some day later we will understand."

"I know," I said, agreeing. "But there is something else on my mind. I can't imagine returning to my old life. It's as if it's finished, it's almost as if I had died, if you understand what I mean. Now I have chosen to live a new life—I was thinking of entering the monastery!"

Father Bede lifted his eyebrows in surprise. "It is a very important decision, entering the monastery," he said, rubbing his chin as if considering my decision.

"But I have already decided, Father Bede," I said with desperation, sitting bolt upright in my chair. "There's nothing else I want to do than live behind the monastery walls! My sister doesn't need my protection any more. She will marry Durwyn. Do you see? Nothing binds me to this world any more! All I wish is to learn to pray and live the life of a monk."

"I understand," Bede said. Yet, he seemed to hesitate. Why did he? Was he not glad that his congregation would gain another soul?

"Before becoming a monk, our men stay in the monastery for a year. During that time they have to get used to this very different life. It's not always easy!" Bede said. "You have to leave everything behind. That is what Jesus recommended his disciples to do. (It is written in the Gospel.) So, the first year is a trial to find out if you're fit for a life of chastity and humility. After that year, if you still think it's the right choice and if you have proved worthy of such a life, you can stay; then follow the vows with which you promise to live this way forever."

I sank back in my chair and sighed. Yes, I thought to myself, that's what I want and I am prepared to take the challenge upon me.

"And these three young men?" Father Bede asked, looking at Erik, Bjorn and Karl. "What is their ambition?"

Erik realised the question was about them. "Have ye already told him?" he asked.

"Not yet," I answered, and then turned to Bede. "These three men want the same as me. They too want to enter monastic life. You see, before we came here we visited the monastery in Cymry. We stayed there for half a day and spoke with the monks. They were dressed in grey robes instead of brown, like you. That monastery made an impression on them, and after a few days they all decided they wanted to become monks."

Father Bede looked them up and down and spoke: "First you need to help your people to build their homes and start a living here. Then you should learn to speak fluent English, and after that time, if you still have the call, you should go and knock at the door of the Cymry monastery."

I translated his words, and even though they nodded and said yes, I felt that they were disappointed. This was not what they wanted to hear. They were ready to enter the monastery straight away.

Erik folded his arms and asked: "What if the grey monks suggest something else? Perhaps they'd take us in right away."

Father Bede waited until I translated. "I know the friars of St David," he said. "They are holy men and they live a very strict monastic life. I am certain they would say the same as me. You need to mature in order to enter the monastery. And you need the language."

"Fine. We'll use that time for learning yer language then," Karl and Bjorn nodded in agreement. "Of course we're gonna help our people build their homes…"

"Yes, and in that time you shall learn more about God and the Christian religion, which you haven't known until now," Bede concluded.

"Will you let me enter now?" I asked Bede impatiently. Perhaps my procedure would be faster, I thought. I was, after all, already a Christian and knew a lot more than my Viking friends.

"I need to talk with you," he answered. "You can stay here overnight and pray about your calling. Let them know that they too need to pray. They should pray every day to our one true God. I would say it may take a year before it is time for them to knock on the door of the grey monks." Then we turned to another subject and Father Bede asked the three if they knew about more Viking invasions in Mercia.

Erik said: "He has to know that attacks are going to happen on this land," he instructed. "But we don't know when and where exactly."

I translated this to Father Bede. His face turned grey. "Would you be prepared to help our people when they attack?" he asked. The three of them answered eagerly: "Yeah, of course!"

Erik got up from his chair. "Now that we've got to know ye, we will not let any harm come upon ye." He held up a fist in the air. "What a disgrace to slaughter innocent men who don't do any harm and don't even own weapons to defend themselves!"

"Ye can count on us any time," Bjorn promised, while Karl added, "We have learned to become warriors, but we won't use it for useless attacks."

Father Bede swiped his hand in the air as if he'd want to wipe away the threat of a Viking invastion. "For now, go back to your people and help them build up a living," he said. "Let's hope your defence won't be needed. But may God's will be done…"

"Right, now let's learn as much of the Anglo-Saxon language as we can," Karl exclaimed.

Father Bede led us to the door. "And remember, the most important preparation for entering a monastery is to pray and pray. Pray to our Lord Jesus Christ, he is the one who calls you."

Bede had said all they needed to know for the moment, and now it would be up to the three to do as they were told.

"When you go back to the others," I told Erik, Bjorn and Karl, "tell them I have an important matter to discuss here in the monastery, and therefore I will stay on for a bit."

"Does Rohanna know ye wanna become a monk?" Erik asked.

I shook my head. "First I have to know whether the monks are going to accept me. If they do, I will explain everything and say goodbye, before I turn my back on the world."

"Sounds as if yer gonna die," Bjorn said, grinning.

"Of course I'm not dying," I replied. "But to become a monk, I must leave the world behind me."

I was certain that I didn't want to go back to my old life. I saw no reason to go back to modern Britain, and now, here in Mercia, I was going to turn away from the world and retreat behind monastery walls.

Chapter Twenty-Five—Assessment

When the three left for the village, Bede invited me to have supper with the monks. I took a seat at the table between two monks who served me before themselves, piling my plate with cooked barley, leek and carrots with cheese, and later with apple puree and roasted chopped hazelnuts.

At the end of the meal, Bede approached me and said: "In order to reflect on your idea of living in the monastery, you may take part in our evening prayers, the Vespers. For Vespers we gather in the chapel—you will hear the bell ringing when it's time. After that you can stay overnight in the same cell you stayed in last time. Lauds is the early morning prayer. It will take place at 5 o'clock. When the chapel bell wakes you, you'll have half an hour to get ready." He then raised his voice for all to hear and said a prayer of thanksgiving. "Now begins a time of silence," he said as he nodded a brief goodbye to me and left the dining room.

After that there was no talking. The monks remained silent as they removed the dishes from the table and each withdrew from the dining room. After sunset, the bell rang and we all silently gathered in the chapel. The chapel resounded with the monks chanting, and I asked myself how long it would take until I'd know the songs and prayers by heart.

It had turned dark by the time Vespers was over. The monks left the chapel in silence and one by one they vanished behind their cell doors. One of the monks accompanied me to my cell, illuminating the way with a small oil lamp. The room was at the end of the corridor before it turned a corner. He lit another oil lamp to stand on the table before leaving with a nod. The room hadn't changed since I had spent the night here a few years ago, when I was on my quest to fight Ethón. A warm breeze blew through the open window. At least now there would be no terror at night, I thought. Ethón was besieged and Mercia was free.

But then I remembered that the country was not free from the other threat. I thought of the Vikings, and how terrifying their attacks were. I remembered from history that the Vikings were one of the threats people feared most in the early Middle Ages. Viking men went berserk and slaughtered everyone they came across. And those women and men they didn't kill were taken away and forced into slavery. With a shudder I thought of the friary. Monasteries were often one of the first places to be attacked. In the museum we had visited in Norway, I remembered viewing images showing attacks on monasteries like this one. The monks were easy prey, and the few precious items they possessed, such as golden chalices and silver crosses embedded with precious stones, were attractive loot for the Vikings. They'd burn any books they'd find—books which took the monks years to write—and they'd destroy the market gardens.

"Excalibur!" The name of the sword shot through my head. The sword! I wondered if it was still here—the sword with which I had fought against Ethón. The sword which had saved Mercia from the terrors of Ethón. Wouldn't now be the time to use it again, when raiding Vikings were coming? The monks would never use violence themselves. They were only the guardians of Excalibur. But who would help them, if danger was approaching? Once again, there was a calling in me: "You need to help them," the inward voice said. But I didn't want to hear it. Hadn't I decided to live a new life, to turn away from the world and enter the monastery?

"Excalibur!" I heard again. It wasn't letting go of me. I heard "Excalibur!" when I lay down, tired, wanting to sleep, and "Excalibur!" followed me into my sleep.

In the morning I awoke with the sun shining directly through the cracks in the bolted door.

But morning hadn't driven out my thoughts of Excalibur. I felt an urge to help fight off the potential invasion, more than I felt the calling to become a monk. If the marauding Vikings were near, this monastery would be one of their targets. Remembering again the visit we paid to the museum in Norway, wasn't it exactly this monastery that was pictured, or was I fantasising?

I wasn't sure about becoming a monk, but what else was I going to do with my life? I was without orientation. If I really wanted to become a monk, surely I should be more convinced and persistent? Perhaps I wasn't made for monastic life after all. Weakened by these doubts, I got on my knees to pray. It was already late. I had missed morning prayers. I had heard the bell in my sleep, but had dozed off again. Now the monks were already coming out of the chapel. There was a soft knock on my door.

One of the monks asked: "Are you ready for breakfast? Father Bede would like to talk to you afterwards. Meet him in his study."

I didn't feel like eating, and I dreaded the talk with Father Bede. Yesterday, I had been full of enthusiasm for leaving the world behind; but now, I wasn't sure any more. Straw fire. Like a youth, I had been quickly enthusiastic about becoming a monk, but the next moment the fire had died down. What would I tell Father Bede?

For breakfast there was fried egg, flat barley bread and water to drink. The monks didn't speak much at table, and I was glad about that. I didn't want to share any of my thoughts and doubts. These monks had vowed to stay in the monastery for their whole life; they had made a decision, perhaps by overcoming doubts or having none at all. But I didn't have this conviction.

After swallowing the water in my ceramic mug, I stood up to join in thanksgiving with everyone else. I wished I could switch off my thoughts and just say prayers day and night and work the way the monks did. *Ora et labora...* But the voice in my head wouldn't keep quiet: "Excalibur!" resounded in my head. "Help the monks!" Yesterday I had been looking forward to becoming a monk; but today I knew I wasn't going to live with them, even if I wished to. I had become angry inside, angry at God, angry at life. Why wasn't life the way I wished it to be?

I found Father Bede in his study where a few other monks were silently copy-writing from large books, each sitting at their own small desk. Bede was overlooking their work, and when I entered he came up and led me to a corner out of hearing from the others. There was a slight smile and sparkle in his eye. He was probably looking forward to hearing my positive decision.

"How are you today?" he asked.

I took a deep breath. "I may not be ready for entering the monastery after all," I answered, suppressing my angry feelings. I thought he'd be disappointed, but instead he smiled even more than before.

"That is quite usual with young men," he said. "You see, it is important to distinguish between escaping and having a call. If you only want to enter a monastery in order to escape from your own life, then it will not last. A proper calling to become a monk is strong and steady."

I nodded in agreement and held my head in my hands. "But now, I don't know what to do with my life. I need to rethink it all over again."

I probably sounded ridiculous, but Bede didn't give me that feeling.

"I thought as much," Father Bede said, pointing in the air then tapping his chin and looking around, as if to confirm that nobody was listening. "I would like you to meet someone."

I sighed. I didn't really want to meet anyone now, I wanted to be alone to sort out my thoughts. "Could I just stay for a few days and think about my life?" I asked. And then it poured out of me: "You see, I was once married—my wife died. It's a long time ago ... you need to know that even though I'm young, I have lived for decades in that other place where I come from. And now, I just want to begin a new life. But it seems that God doesn't want me to do it. He's calling me to help you—not as a monk, but as a fighter. Just as I was before, when I was called to defeat Ethón. Could it be that he wants me to help protect you from Viking invasions?"

Bede closed his eyes for a few seconds and took a deep breath. If he hadn't already thought I was mad before, he probably did now.

"Yes," he said, "I do think God is calling you." He was serious. "And now," he continued, "follow me to the visitors' room."

Reluctantly, I got up and followed him. I had no idea who was awaiting me. Maybe he had called for a doctor for madness.

Before I entered, he took another deep breath and said: "I will leave you now. You may enter on your own." Without another word, he turned away and left the building. For a second I thought of doing the same—turning around and walking not only out of this building, but away from the monastery, on and on, away from everything. But something inside me forced me to take hold of the bolt and I pushed open the door.

Chapter Twenty-Six—Another Reunion

There, sitting on a chair, was a young girl. I saw her from the side and it looked as if she had been looking through the window, deep in thought. But when she saw me come in, she got up and turned around. Then we both froze.

"Veronica!" I burst out. "Why, how … is it possible?"

In front of me stood my late wife. But she was alive and well. Her brown skin was immaculate, without creases, and her smile was as youthful as it had been years ago. Her dark frizzy hair was tied back, and she had not a single grey hair. Her eyes shone lovingly.

"How can this be?" I repeated. I didn't dare to step closer. "Are you real… I mean, aren't you just an apparition?"

She laughed and her voice sounded fresh and smooth. My heart jumped from the sudden rush of happiness.

"Of course I'm real!" she said, reaching out her hand. I took it. It felt warm and gentle. I studied her face, and my heart filled with warmth. This was my wife, no doubts at all, but she was young again, about seventeen years old.

"So there is a life after death!" I whispered, my eyes fixed on her face.

"Did you ever doubt it?" she asked.

"I wasn't always sure…"

"It's easier to believe in an afterlife than in another world, I guess," she said, chuckling the way she always used to.

"Look how young you are!" I said, touching her cheek.

153

"What about you?" she asked, grinning.

"Have I changed?"

"You're much younger ... but very much the same."

"You too. You haven't changed much either," I answered.

Then we both chuckled and shed tears and laughed again. Veronica was back—I didn't want to let go of her hand. Time and space vanished around us. I didn't think of where I was nor about the inner conflict I had just been through. Now there were no questions any more: Veronica was back in my life, and there was nothing else I wanted.

"How did you get here?" I asked, puzzled.

"It's a strange story, but you're used to unusual stories, aren't you?" she said, hinting at the times I used to tell her about Mercia. I never found out if Veronica believed in what Rohanna and I had experienced as children. She used to listen carefully, but it was a very strange story, and it seemed she couldn't make up her mind whether to believe it or not. After a while, I used to avoid the subject.

But now she was here herself.

"Remember the moment I died?" she asked as we both sat down, holding hands.

"Yes, you were very weak and wasted. I was holding your hand, just as I'm holding it now. It was limp," I swallowed, "and I felt so heavy..."

Veronica nodded. "My eyes were closed," she said. "I couldn't open them any more. I wanted to say something to you, but I was unable to. Your voice became distant, and soon I couldn't hear you any more... That's when I realised I had left my body, left you, left the world. At the same time I was completely awake. First, I entered into complete darkness, but just for a short moment. Then I saw a light approaching: a strong light, stronger than the sun. But strangely, I could look into the light without a problem. I wondered where this light came from and what it was, and so I walked towards it—yes, I was walking although I had left my body.

154

"The light was warm and friendly, and I felt loved, as if by a very loving person, but I didn't see anyone. Following the light, I walked through a stone arch with white and red roses growing around it. The light shone from beyond the arch. As soon as I passed through it, the shining light disappeared, but the place was still bright and I could still feel the warmth and love from the light. Then I discovered that I was stepping on grass, and when I looked down I realised that I was in my body, but I didn't feel weak or ill any more. I was as healthy and fresh as if I'd never had any physical issues."

"What kind of place had you reached?"

"All I can say is that it was beautiful, and the roses smelt stronger than earthly ones. In front of me, the view wasn't clear. As if through a mist, I vaguely saw someone walking around, and then two or three more. Then my vision became clearer and I noticed I was standing in a garden. I saw circular flowerbeds, cultivated bushes and trees… The mist vanished, and when I looked back at the arch with the roses, it had gone too. There was just a bare stone wall with a black gate. The people who were walking around were monks in brown robes. They were at work in the garden, cutting bushes, picking berries, watering vegetables. I went up to them and asked what kind of place this was, and they seemed amazed to see me. I wasn't sure if their surprise was because of my looks or my question. 'This is the Hamberton friary,' one of them said. And then I remembered your tale from childhood and I realised this must be Mercia, the place that you and Rohanna had talked about."

"So, you finally believe it now?" I said with a surprised grin.

"Well, I'm here now, so there's no option but to believe it!" she said as we both grinned.

There was a gentle knock on the door—Father Bede was back.

"What are you planning to do now?" he asked, smiling with a twinkle in his eye.

I rose from my chair. "You have given me a big surprise!" I answered, still in shock.

"Your wife was already here before you arrived. She's been staying in the monastery for two days and has told us her story. It is a miraculous story, inexplicable, but God can do unimaginable things."

"So when I came here the second time, she was here, but you didn't tell me when I was considering becoming a monk?"

Bede nodded. "Yes, because I wanted you to make a voluntary decision. If you had seen your wife before you let go of wanting to become a monk, you would have felt forced to be with her. The brothers and I prayed for you—I trusted that God would come up with the right solution."

Veronica looked at me with raised eyebrows. "You wanted to become a monk?" she asked.

"Not any more. A woman has come in between!" I said, grinning and taking her hand again.

"Adrian had his doubts this morning," Bede said. "He seemed to have turned away from the idea of becoming a monk. I saw this as a sign from God that it was time to bring you to him."

Father Bede turned to me. "So, will you now return together to Durwyn's village?"

"Yes," I said, reassured. There was no question of that. Now I understood why I hadn't wanted to become a monk after all. Veronica was with me and our life would resume together in Mercia. But there was one more thing I needed to know: "What has happened to Excalibur?" I asked.

Bede nodded and beckoned us to follow him. He led us along the corridor, past the dozen cell doors, until we arrived once more at the room with the scribes. Behind this room lay a small room which we entered. It was dark inside, with only a tiny window under the ceiling that let in a faint light. There was a metal case decorated with fragments of transparent glass, and inside it lay Excalibur in its shaft, embossed with blue stones. Bede opened the case and indicated with a wave of his hand that I should pick up the sword.

I carefully lifted it from its purple padding, pulled it out of its shaft and admired it from all sides. The golden blade had been polished, and the haft sparkled as it had when I first received it in the chapel. I thought about the power which lay in the sword and how it had helped me fight Ethón, ending the terror which had reigned over Mercia.

"Excalibur, the sword made for King Arthur by the most skilled blacksmiths of Mercia," Father Bede described it to Veronica. Then he turned to me, lowered his voice and almost whispered: "You may soon need it again. With the Vikings attacking different parts of the country— God knows when it will be our turn…"

He closed the case and said: "Take the sword with you. A young husband needs his own weapon. In Mercia it is unheard of for a man to be without his sword."

Without a word, I slipped the sword back into its sheath. Bede produced a belt from a shelf underneath the case which I tied around my waist. Once again I had become the bearer of Excalibur.

"This time, Excalibur may remain in your possession as long as you live," Father Bede announced. Then he sprinkled the sword with blessed water, as well as Veronica and me, while praying in Latin.

Now it was time to leave for the village, and I couldn't wait to show Veronica everything, and to introduce her to everyone there.

The sun began to set as we walked through the tussocks of heather. The golden red rays lit the millions of purple flower heads, transforming them into a sea of gold and blue. My heart too was like a sea of gold. Now Veronica was back, my loneliness had come to an end. I could look forward to building a house for ourselves in Durwyn's village.

Excalibur hung at my side; I now belonged to the brigade of sword holders. During our walk, I told Veronica about our journey around the globe: how we'd ended up in Norway and decided to go back to England; how we got lost in the fog and then met our Viking friends; the adventures we had on the boat journey through the fjords and out to the open sea; how we met the Picts and later the Welsh monks, and then eventually set up camp close to Hamberton.

I told her about my whole life, the two decades that had passed since her death.

"Isn't it strange?" she said. "You've lived through years and years, while for me it seems like only a few days since I passed away."

"So, the time between you leaving our world and arriving at the monastery was short?"

"Yes, well at least that's how it felt. When I passed away and left my body, I followed the light and arrived at the monastery—this may have taken just a few minutes…"

"That's how things work between our old world and this world," I said, recalling how Rohanna and I had been away for five days, while for our mother it had only been twenty minutes.

Then Veronica said: "Adrian, I know this is an awkward question, but where was I buried?"

I stood still, and said: "You don't know?"

"I do know it was at the graveyard on the outside of our little town."

"Yes, they built a new supermarket nearby."

"But the point is, don't you think it's exactly the same place as…"

"As what?"

"Our town was where Hamberton is now. And the graveyard is…"

"The monastery here?"

"Remember, the road was called Friary Road, and we never knew why!"

"You're right. There was no monastery, not even ruins left behind."

"Unless the graveyard was built on the ruins of the monastery…"

"That's possible," I answered in awe. "So when you walked through the arch with the roses…"

"…I was actually stepping from the graveyard into the monastery grounds, as if I was stepping from one time into another time. It's all the same place, but different ages."

"I understand. The place where you were buried was the place that transferred you from modern time to Anglo-Saxon time. And when you arrived here, you were in the same place as the graveyard had been; but instead of the graveyard, there was now a live monastery with monks."

"While years, even decades had passed for you, for me it was only a short time."

"And now we're both here, and we're both young again!" I exclaimed. A rush of energy swept through me. All at once I wanted to run, jump, climb trees and lift my young wife into the air. I embraced Veronica and swung her around as she laughed aloud. When I put her down again, we held hands and ran along the path through the high grass, past the forest edge and skipped over the little brook. Soon, looking down from the hill, we spotted Durwyn's village on the hill beyond, and behind it the hill with the chapel.

"There it is!" I shouted, out of breath. "We're almost there! It's just a twenty-minute walk from here."

"It's beautiful," Veronica said, admiring the view. "Just nature all around, little villages, farmers' fields in harmony with nature. No asphalt roads, no cars, no metal road signs, no concrete and no electric wires, power stations or anything like it. Maybe Mercia is paradise?"

I looked around me. She was right: nature was in harmony with what was man-made. The paths were natural and all the houses were made from organic materials which the villagers had found in the area.

"It's close to paradise," I admitted. "But there are challenges. Mercia's not free from every evil. There are conflicts and wars ... and threats from the Vikings."

My heart began beating louder as we approached the village, and I held Veronica's hand a little tighter.

"So this is Durwyn's village?" she whispered. "At last I'll get to know it!"

"And Rohanna will get to see you too!"

"Do you think I'm going to shock her?" she smiled.

"Rohanna will definitely be surprised—but the villagers not. They never knew you before."

"But they may have never seen a brown-skinned person!" she said.

"How do you know?" I asked. I remembered one of my Viking friends and said: "Karl's as brown as you. Apparently, his mother got pregnant on a voyage to Africa. How did the monks react to your appearance?"

"They asked where I was from. I said I was from England, but they didn't seem to know where that was. After all, they call it Mercia and not England. They told me to follow them and brought me to Bede. Only then did I tell the whole story. It must have sounded crazy, but this was what had happened to me. How else could I explain why I was suddenly here? He didn't really react at all, and I wasn't sure what he was thinking about my incredible story."

"Yes, that's how Bede is. He doesn't say much, but he does listen well."

"Then I found out that he knew you. And he advised me to stay in their monastery until you'd arrive. He assumed you'd be here soon. After explaining where I was from and what had happened to me, he advised me to keep it secret. 'Not everyone would understand these miracles,' he said."

We were now near the fence around the village. I pushed open the gate and whispered to Veronica: "Welcome to the Anglo-Saxon village!" It didn't take long for us to find out where the other travellers were. At the back of the village, in the shade of the oak trees that were growing beyond the fence, stood a group of people talking. As we approached them, I recognised Erik, Bjorn, Karl, Durwyn, Rohanna and four other villagers discussing where the new houses were to be built. Rohanna turned round. She was the first to see the two of us approaching. Puzzled, she looked in my direction, wondering who the woman was accompanying me. And the more she observed, the more puzzled she became, until we were close up when she clasped her hands over her mouth.

Rohanna recognised my wife. It had been a very long time since she and Veronica had seen each other, and especially since they were both young, yet Rohanna recognised her. She stepped out of the group and almost stumbled as she hastened towards us.

"Is it you, Veronica?" she asked in shock. "Can this be?"

"Yes, yes, it is me," Veronica said, smiling.

"But how?"

"We'll explain later," I said hastily. Then they hugged each other. Rohanna looked back and forth from Veronica to me. "You've got your wife back," she said with damp eyes. "I can't believe it!"

"These days, quite a few things are unbelievable," I joked. "It's hard to keep up!" Tears were flowing now for both Veronica and Rohanna, and I admit that I found it difficult to keep my own tears back. It wasn't long before Durwyn's curiosity got the better of him.

"Who is this?" he asked as he joined us.

"This is my young wife!" I said.

"Young? Aren't we all young?"

"I don't take it for granted," I answered, winking at Rohanna and Veronica. Then I introduced her to the others.

Karl, Bjorn and Erik kissed her hand in honour, as if she were a queen, when they heard that she was my wife. A male villager, around fifty years of age, asked her: "Where are you from?"

"My mother's English—I mean Anglo-Saxon," she began to explain. "My father is from, well…" she hesitated and looked at me.

"He's from a warm country in the south," I concluded. They wouldn't have known where South America was. It hadn't been discovered yet by Columbus (although I had heard that Vikings had already travelled there).

"What country of the south is your father from?" the villager asked, and pointing at Karl he asked: "Are you both from the same place? You both have curly dark hair and brown skin colour."

Veronica shook her head. "No," she explained, "Karl's father is from Africa…?" Karl nodded. "But my dad comes from another part of the world," she added.

"It's not yet discovered," slipped from my mouth. The others looked at me, confused.

"What do you mean, not yet discovered?" another villager asked.

"I'm sure the monks know," the first villager replied. "They are educated and know about these things."

"The country my father's from is far away, across the ocean," Veronica tried to help out. "It's very warm all year round, and different plants grow there…"

"I can't imagine a place where it's always warm, even in winter," another villager answered, as we were now surrounded by people. "That must be great!" Someone announced, "Winter is harsh. It makes living hard, especially when there's not enough food."

"All year warm! That must be like paradise," a woman added.

Chapter Twenty-Seven—Village Life

In the following days, our Viking friends who had stayed behind in the camp joined us at the village, and they all dived into learning the language of the Anglo-Saxons. I was astonished how fast they picked up the language. Every day they spoke a few sentences more. At that rate it would take only a few months before they could talk fluently, even if they kept a Norse accent.

We soon began building houses. There was a lot of tree felling, cutting planks and boards, and digging out foundations for our new homes. A part of the village fence at the back was taken down in order to extend the village for the new houses.

Bjorn, Erik and Karl were so engaged with this work that we had no time to talk about their plans for entering the monastery. Yet I believe it was still on their minds. Since Wales, they had turned more serious, with less swearing and quarrelling.

I was excited that Veronica and I were going to have our own little Anglo-Saxon house. Besides the work on building houses, there was other daily work which had to get done: Veronica and I helped out where we could with weeding the gardens, watering when the days were hot and dry, harvesting in the fields, feeding the farm animals, milking cows and goats… Most families had a single cow or a goat or both, which needed milking twice a day. Occasionally a pig or a sheep was butchered and then shared among everyone. A lot of cooking, weaving, spinning and taking care of small children took place throughout the day. Above the age of five, the children didn't really need much looking after. They helped with the work or played by themselves when there was nothing else to do. There were probably around fifteen to twenty children growing up in the village. Youngsters didn't count as children any more, they were treated as adults.

The weather stayed hot and dry for days. But I knew it wouldn't stay like that. Towards the end of September, the sky turned dark grey and heavy clouds emerged. The villagers had worked hard from morning to evening, cutting the meadows. Under their sweat they brought in the grass which had been drying in the hot late summer sun, to store in their barns before the rain poured down. The villagers were tired and irritated after working hard all day, but in the end they were pleased they'd managed to get the grass in before the rain came down. The barns were now filled with hay for their animals, which would get them through the winter. The wheat and barley were now harvested, so the men were busy smoking and salting the meat, and the women slicing vegetables, cabbages, carrots, onions, beetroot, berries, apples and pears and filling them in clay pots as preserves. They put the vegetables in huge pots with salted water for fermenting; the fruit was mixed with honey.

Until our own home was ready, Veronica and I lived in Durwyn's hut, and our Viking friends shared housing in other villagers' homes before the newly built huts were ready to move into.

It was at the end of a hard working day that a messenger from a nearby village came by with devastating news.
He was out of breath as he knocked on a few of the doors. He must have been running most of the way to bring his message. The villagers came out to hear the news, and then called everyone to gather in the hall. It only took a few minutes until most of us were gathered.

Then the messenger raised his voice and spoke:

"Friends, these are the days we have long dreaded. After living now for three years in peace, it has come to our ears that there have been Viking raids on the nearest coast. Whole villages have come under attack, young women robbed of their dignity by violent men who have killed most of the villagers. Those who weren't murdered have been chained and taken away as slaves. This is terrible news, my friends!

"What can be done? Some of us will have lost relatives or friends. And it's not over. The enemy will not stop there. They are coming further into the country with new attacks. This means that Hamberton and the nearby villages are under threat. And be prepared, as these vicious Vikings come at night, or in the early morning before sunrise, when you're sleeping deeply." He flung his arms up in the air, and shouted: "Oh, great God, save us!" Then he sat down and took a sip of mead to relieve his voice.

The listeners' faces were drawn with worry and panic. They murmured in discomfort. The murmuring turned into exclamations. A man called out: "We need to be alert at all times and defend ourselves!"

"We must have someone always awake and on guard!" another said.

Then Bard spoke up, in his simple English, which he had acquired in the past weeks: "We will fight on your side as hard as we can. We are Norse ourselves, and experienced warriors. You have been good to us, and you have given us the new faith. Together with all men of the villages, we will fight against any Viking invasion!"

"We are grateful," said another man. "But how many Vikings do you expect are going to attack?"

"It varies," the messenger said. "They come in groups with around two dozen men, or in larger hordes of up to *two hundred* men!"

A strong wind tore at the walls of the hall, and the rain hammered against the wooden planks. Summer was resisting the onset of Autumn. Summer had come to an end but didn't want to leave, and Autumn was pushing through, making way for colder days.

"How can we let each other know when there is danger of an attack?" another villager asked.

The messenger stood up again. "By the sound of the horn. Whenever you hear a horn blowing several times from across the hill, take it as the sign. As soon as you recognise the warning, pass it on. Take your horn," he said and took his drinking horn of mead in his hand and held it to his mouth to demonstrate. "Blow three times, pause, blow three times again. Repeat that until you hear the next village doing the same. That way we can pass on a warning to each other."

There was a stew cooking over the fire, and when it was ready, a few women ladled the stew into bowls which the villagers had brought with them. There was no meat roasting on the spit this time; we weren't having a feast. Today was an emergency gathering, with nothing to celebrate. But nonetheless we ate ourselves full and drank to the health of the messenger. When the wind calmed down and the rain lessened, he made his way back, before dark.

Chapter Twenty-Eight—The Wedding

It took several weeks of hard work to construct the wooden huts and to fit them out with thick layers of straw for the thatched roofs. Towards the end of October, our new homes were finished. Veronica had got used to life in the village. Compared to living in modern England, there was now much less comfort. Even though I did a lot more physical work on a daily basis, I felt stronger and healthier than I used to. Nature was all around us, and a lot of work too.

When our roof was completed, the beds were fitted around the walls. They were low on the ground without legs, made of wood planks and a wooden frame covered with layers of straw and hay. We used sheepskin for the beds on top, given us by one neighbour; while two other neighbours gave us three cauldrons for the fireplace. From the ceiling hung herbs for drying, which we picked ourselves. Our house was a little smaller than the house of Durwyn's parents. In five steps you could walk across it, and there were no windows. The oak wood of the freshly made entrance door was still light, and a villager showed me how to carve swirling patterns in the door frame, just as on all the other houses. As soon as I completed my carving (it took longer than an experienced carver), Veronica painted the swirls with yellow, red and blue paint (another neighbour instructed her how to make the paint from plant and bark).

Life went on undisturbed, and we almost forgot about the Viking threat. When Veronica and I moved into our house, a priest came to bless all the new homes. He sprinkled the walls with blessed water, while murmuring prayers over us and for our homes. Rohanna had moved into the house where Durwyn's mother and his little sister lived. Since Rohanna and Durwyn weren't married yet, they weren't allowed to live under the same roof until their marriage was sealed. And there *were* marriage plans! The great day was planned for the end of October, and would take place in the chapel, yes the very same chapel which had brought her and me to Mercia for the first time!

"I am excited," Rohanna confessed when I met her one time working in the garden. "But it's strange getting married when none of our family will be there for the wedding."

"Well, I'm here," I answered, tapping my chest. "Veronica's here too, and besides us, a whole bunch of Vikings." We both laughed.

"Yes, they make up for everything," she concluded. And she was right, the Vikings had become family. We had been together through thick and thin, and we had begun a new life here together in the village. Working hard and building together had bonded us, and the results were solid wooden houses for Bard and his wife, Ljot and his family, and Veronica and me.

Bjorn, Erik and Karl lived in Bard's house. Twice they walked all the way to Wales to visit the monks. They hadn't given up on the idea of entering the monastery there; in fact, they became more serious about it. Bard and Helga weren't too enthusiastic about it, though.

"Why would they do such a mad thing and leave everyone behind?" Bard said. But the more he shook his head, the more the three longed to enter monastic life. A priest from Hamberton came to the village once a week to talk with them. We heard them speak about God. They discussed how God had made this world, how Christ was born to save humanity, that every living thing was made by Him, and what it meant to live a pious life, and so forth.

Goda was working on a wedding dress for weeks. It was a linen dress embroidered with flowers, such as poppies, lilies, marguerites and bluebells, and trimmed with gold thread along the sleeves and neckline. I could hardly believe it was all hand-made. The dress wasn't new—it had been worn by other brides before, including Goda. But she had washed it thoroughly, mended weak parts and repaired some of the flowers.

The wedding day arrived and Rohanna wore the flowery dress, now also embellished with red and blue ribbons. It fitted her well, as if it were made for her. It reached down to her ankles, where her feet were clad in light brown leather sandals. Her long red hair was tied in plaits wrapped around her head, and to top it all she bore a wreath of golden wheat ears, entwined with yellow, purple and red dried field flowers.

The chapel bell rang while a procession of villagers— led by the priest and Rohanna and Durwyn, closely followed by Goda, Fridogitha, Veronica and myself— strode up the hill to the chapel where the wedding ceremony was to take place. The chapel was decorated with bundles of wheat and field flowers. As we flocked into the chapel, we filled to the brim. The door was left open so that more could participate from outside. The priest laid his stole, the band which hung around the back of his neck and over his shoulders, above the couple's hands. They promised to be faithful to each other, to love one another and to care for each other their whole life long, after which the priest sealed the marriage with his blessing.

Afterwards, the crowd gathered outside. The priest dipped a stick in a metal basin and sprinkled holy water over us. Musicians playing string instruments, drums, tambourines, bells and flutes escorted the procession down the narrow path, through the tall grass and all the way back to the village, where a great feast was prepared in the hall.

It seemed like every known dish was laid out that day: roasted meat, salted and pickled fish, fried fish, pickled vegetables, honey-sweetened pastry and berry mixtures, eggs—pickled, fried, scrambled and boiled—cooked barley grains with diced vegetables and roasted nuts were just some of it. There were so many dishes and treats that I could hardly remember them all.

Our Norse friends, as well as Veronica and I, were introduced to Durwyn's relatives—his uncles, cousins, aunts, uncles and their families who had come from other villages. I also spotted two monks from Hamberton who had come to give their blessings; they left shortly after being served with mead and pastry. I also saw the old lady we'd met at the market. The guests gave the newlyweds presents—small furniture, pots of preserved food, jewellery and weapons.

The day ended with a glorious sunset. As the sky turned dark pink-red, the air cooled down and people packed their things to leave for home. When it was dark, everyone disappeared into their huts. The tidying up would follow next day, when it was daylight again.

Now that Rohanna was married, none of us had to worry about the other twin being lonely. We lived near each other in the same village, and both of us were happy.

But then, two days after the wedding, Veronica woke me in the middle of the night. With a worried voice, she said: "Do you hear that?"

"Hmm?" I responded. Surely it wasn't time to get up yet.

"It sounds like the horn!"

"Which horn?" I asked drowsily. Then, within seconds, I understood which horn she meant.

Chapter Twenty-Nine—Attack

The sound of the horns came from the direction of Hamberton. Day hadn't yet broken and I wanted to carry on sleeping, but knew that I couldn't. Overcoming my drowsiness, I got out of bed and splashed cold water on my face to freshen up. Other men were quicker than me, and I heard them gathering outside. It took me a few more minutes to get ready. Excalibur lay ready behind my bed. Veronica squeezed my hand tightly as I left.

Around a dozen men, including Durwyn, Karl, Bjorn and Erik, were waiting outside. They carried swords at their sides, and some of them a round wooden shield. A faint light showed on the eastern horizon where the sun would rise. Some stars were still visible, especially the morning star. Others were fading away as the sun came up. The men hardly spoke. I didn't feel like talking either. Nervously, I held my sword tight and thought of what was to come. It was many years since I had fought Ethón, the beast. Yet, how could I be sure the sword would help me now? I wasn't a warrior, I had never learnt to fight properly. But now there was little time to think or to change my mind. One of the older men began hitting his sword against the wood of his shield.

"Ready to move?" he croaked.

Everyone, apart from me, answered with a firm "Yes!"

"Those in front are those in full armour; followed by those with shields; and those with only swords remain at the back," he ordered.

I belonged to the last group. My heart beat strongly. I suppressed my fear. The gathering broke up. Too much time to think would just give us more opportunity to become anxious and imagine things. All we needed was the spirit of bravery!

Some of the village women stood silently at the entrance to their huts, watching us leave. An elderly man who was unfit for fighting came up to the group, crossed himself several times and said: "May God bless and protect you! May he bestow on you strength and bravery!"

Several of the men responded with "Amen!"

Then the leader of the group beat his shield a final time. "Off we go!" he roared, and the group marched off through the gate and down the hill. We were around sixteen men, between the age of 16 and 45. We marched fast, almost at a jog. The landscape was all in shades of black and grey, as it was still quite dark. We sometimes stumbled as there was not enough light to see well. I closed my eyes —it wasn't much different from walking with eyes open. Perhaps this was just a dream—a nightmare from which I'd wake up soon. I shook my head; it was all real. I felt the cold breeze in my face, and gradually the sky brightened as the day broke. A flock of birds screeched from the sky as they gathered for their flight to a warmer country; they had better things to do than fight each other.

After an hour of silent walking, the monastery walls appeared. The air was cold, but walking had kept us warm. The sun shone down between grey clouds. There was grey mist rising from the ground, and the cool droplets dampened our faces.

"See, there's smoke coming from the buildings," one of the men exclaimed. We all stopped in our tracks.

"That can't mean anything good," another said. It didn't look like harmless cooking smoke rising from a fireplace. The grey coils turned black and heavy and they darkened the morning sky, as if it had turned night again.

We clustered into a tight group. Words were exchanged between the leader and a few of the men in low voices, and then the leader raised a call.

"Uraghhhhh!" he growled with all his might, and the others joined in, "Uraghhh! Uraghhhh! Heeeeeeyyyyy!"

It was the call of attack, the war cry. Nobody needed to tell me—it roused the embers of bravery awaiting deep in each of us. I grabbed my sword and joined in the cry,

"Uraghhh! Heyyeyeeey!"

Every cell in my body seemed to vibrate as my cry mingled with the cries of the other men. Then the leader started running, sword in the air, shield in front of him, closely followed by everyone else behind, including me.

I sweated from the run, but this was no time to stop, and certainly no time to reflect. Everything was happening fast. We arrived at the burning monastery like a wild pack of growling wolves. I could hardly recognise the place, which had always been so silent and peaceful. Now, everywhere showed destruction: doors were torn off, tables knocked over, beds and crosses ripped out of place. The chapel door was wide open, revealing flames that had reached the ceiling. We heard glass bursting. Dense smoke billowed from the window openings and gushed skywards, stinging our eyes and throats. We coughed and jumped aside, gasping for fresh air.

I almost tripped. At my feet lay a dead body, deeply wounded and head separated. I let out a screech. And then I discovered more, scattered here and there, deeply wounded, with body parts missing. None of them were Vikings. The monks had been meek and weaponless—an easy prey. I stared at the corpse I had tripped over and turned away, terrified. I wanted to leave—get out of here as fast as possible. Retreating backwards, I almost stumbled over another dead body. I glanced down. The face looked too familiar. A cold shudder swept through my heart. I knew who it was: Father Bede. They had killed him, along with several other brothers.

"We've come too late!" I shouted in despair.

"Watch out!" Bard shouted back. "There! Look over there!" A Viking spotted us and bawled to his fellow warriors. They came running and jumping out of every corner, shouting wildly, swords raised in the air, ready to smash everything to bits. We were sixteen men, but the Vikings were in the majority, perhaps double as many. I gripped my sword as fiercely as I could, preparing for combat.

The words they shouted, I couldn't understand. They sounded like horrible grunts mixed with laughter: the greedy laughs of an evil victory. As they sprang at us, Bard was the first to clash with a Viking. The frontline of our warriors fought bravely. I heard the slashing and yelling as the fight was close. Soon the Vikings had burst through our frontline, exposing first the middle and then the backline. Out of nowhere, a Viking sprang at me. Within seconds, and before I had the chance to defend myself, I received a strong and painful blow on my left shoulder. My sword fell from me and slid under an overturned table. I landed on my face, hit my nose, and dripping with blood, I awaited the unmerciful strike of the Viking's sword which would end my life.

But instead, someone grabbed my wrists and ankles roughly and fastened them in chains. With a few kicks in my side, I was rolled along the gravel path, my skin scraping on the stones. This rough journey ended on the grass, next to a few others who were chained in the same way. My face was pressed downwards in the grass, which at least soothed my injured nose and wounded face. I was unable to turn, yet longed to get up. Sweat and dirt stuck to my hair and face. I breathed deeply, trying to make out what this all meant.

There were others next to me, tied up in the same manner: perhaps around five villagers and two or three monks. I couldn't see my Norse friends. We were guarded by a thick bearded Viking who rested his foot on one of the captured men, as if he was a log.

What had happened to Erik, Bjorn and Karl? Were they lying somewhere dead on the ground? Or had they fled? I turned my head to try to recognise those lying closest to me. There were monks also tied in chains, unable to get up. Face down, they looked worried and yet strangely peaceful, as if they'd accepted their fate. A wave of anger rose up in me as I saw how these defenceless men were being treated. But my anger was useless. I was weak and captured. And I had lost Excalibur, the sword which had protected me from Ethón, the sword that King Arthur had fought with in war. I felt useless. I had hardly fought one bit today. If I died now, there would be nothing honourable about my death. In the background I heard shouts and more vicious laughs coming from our attackers. All our men had either fled, were killed or were lying tied down like me.

Chapter Thirty—At the River Bank

My wrists hurt from the pressure of the chains. But I felt even more pain piercing my heart. Lying on the ground, unable to do anything, and just waiting for whatever the Vikings would decide to do with us, I thought of Father Bede. I had seen him lying dead on the ground, his head smeared with blood, with dark blood stains on his brown habit, especially across his chest. He might have been stabbed in the heart. His head was turned sideways, eyes shut, mouth open. Blood had seeped from his mouth and was already drying on the ground.

I closed my eyes. Father Bede, the father and guardian of this monastery, was gone forever. Dead. And with him, some other monks too. Any who had survived were captured and tied up like me. The monastery that I had known for so long was wrecked within just a few hours.

Two of the Vikings approached us. "Get up, get up!" they shouted in their hoarse voices. Roughly, they released the chains around our ankles, only to tie them again differently: now all of us were chained together, one captive behind the other. "Heads down!" We were forced to stare at the ground.

"Move, move!" came the next order. And move we did. Heads down, shoulders sunken—a miserable group of men, driven by shouting Vikings. As soon as one of us stopped or looked up, he got kicked or thumped. When we stumbled and tripped—it was not easy to walk in chains—a torrent of swear words came from one of the Vikings, accompanied by an arbitrary blow.

As we trod on, fear filled my soul. How and where would we end up? What if they took us somewhere far away? I wouldn't have the chance to tell Veronica. I was desperate to talk to someone. Chained in front of me was a monk. Perhaps he had a clue what this all meant.

"Do you hear me?" I whispered, when the two Vikings weren't close enough to overhear.

"Yes, I hear you," he replied under strain.

"What are they going to do with us? Why didn't they finish us off right away?"

"Most probably," he began and coughed, "they'll want to take us to their country ... far away. We are their captured, free work force. That's what we are for them..."

One of the Vikings drew closer. "Get on, get on, you bastards!" he bellowed. We shut up and kept our heads down.

The clouds covered the sun. A chilly autumn wind blew around our ears.

The Vikings chewed dry meat during the walk and drank mead from their skin bottles, but we didn't get anything. My throat was dry and my stomach began to grumble, while they gulped down their refreshments. As we stumbled along stony paths and field tracks, the maltreatment continued. With punches, kicks and shouts they showed us who was now boss. The walk seemed to go on forever, and we didn't know where it was leading.

It must have taken a few hours—most it spent in silence, for there was hardly a chance to communicate with fellow captives without expecting blows from our captors.

My feet hurt from the chain around my ankles and from having to take such small steps. My neck was in pain from holding my head down most of the time and my shoulder ached from the sword blow of earlier. I tried not to think about it. Weren't we all suffering the same? Perhaps for others this trial was even worse. A couple of monks seemed to be struggling from the hardship. But when a captor came close, they tried to appear strong and sturdy. "If you want to stay alive, don't show signs of weakness," someone called from behind, when it was safe to speak. "If you look weak, they will think you're useless and make short work of you." I understood why they had picked the strongest looking men.

What was better? I asked myself. To be taken away to a foreign country and spend the rest of one's life as a slave, or rather die straight away? There must be another option! Escape … escape…! But how? At least one of us should escape and tell the others in the village what had happened to the rest. Somebody should let them know which shore we are heading for, before we were shipped off. Somebody needed to tell my wife, Veronica. These worries occupied my thoughts as we reached a river bank, where six longboats were tied up to poles, rocking in the rippling water. Each longboat had plentiful space for around thirty men, altogether they could carry at least 180 warriors. With so many men, it was not surprising that they were able to raid our villages.

The clouds now covered the sky completely, and the sun was nearing the horizon. As it was autumn, days were short and soon it would be dark.

"Sit down!" one of the Vikings barked, gesticulating with his hands. We settled down in the grass, which was coarse and wet. There were now dozens of Vikings passing us, going back and forth. Some commented as they spotted us crouched on the ground. They suggested prices for how much we were worth, and shared ideas of how they'd make use of us in their own country. Others were busy dragging heavy sacks and boxes, which I assumed were filled with loot—stolen items from the villages and monastery. Some made camp fires to keep warm, and started roasting meat. The smell reached my nose und made me even hungrier.

Before it was completely dark, I noticed another group of captured figures arriving. The group sat down a few metres away from us, their backs turned. Both groups were guarded by a Viking. One or the other occasionally turned his head in our direction. That was when I noticed Durwyn among them. The moment he spotted me too, we nodded to each other. Not only had Veronica lost me, but Rohanna too would be left without her husband. Without exchanging words, we knew the heavy thoughts that were weighing us down.

Next to me sat a villager resting his head on his knees.

"There must be a way to escape this," I murmured, only loud enough for those near me to hear.

"How?" he whispered back. "We're trapped by these chains and how brutal these men are. We've lost the battle. And with it our homes … our family, our wives, our children. Be prepared," he said with a deep sigh, "you may never see them again. We are now slaves!"

"We must defend ourselves, even if just with words! Perhaps by reasoning we could win them over!" I answered.

The villager looked up and let out a short, cynical chuckle. "You want to debate with these mad men? Haven't you seen how ruthless they are? There is no way we can defend ourselves. They've taken all our weapons. We are utterly defenceless!" he said and dropped his head back on his knees.

I stared down at the river. As far as I could tell, back in modern Britain, this would be the River Severn. It flowed through a city called Gloucester before reaching the sea. How long would it take to get to the open sea from here? Perhaps an hour? As long as we were on the river, I could jump off the boat and try to swim … but only if we weren't tied down with chains. Yet, what an easy prey I'd be if they caught me swimming near the boat. And once we were at sea, there'd be no way to escape. I thought of our adventurous voyage with all challenges and effort it had taken to get here from Norway. We had left everything behind to come to Mercia with our Norse friends. Had it all been for nothing?

The sun's last rays vanished behind the river bank, making way for heavy clouds that spread out across the evening sky. Darkness enveloped the place. I shuddered. I wasn't only feeling cold—an inner emptiness made me lose hope. I was exhausted and traumatised from the battle and the strain of the last few hours. I closed my eyes and wished I could drift away from all the misery. Perhaps I could go to sleep and never wake up again. "No!" I said to myself, and brushed away the temptation of giving in to despair.

Just then I heard a shout in the Norse language. A man holding a burning torch came near. The torch barely lit his face—he used the light to examine his surroundings, and it scanned over us, illuminating the two groups of men huddled on the ground for a brief moment. Our captors stood in the background, apparently having a meal and talking with their mouths full to the man holding the torch.

We were given no food, and a whole day had passed since I had eaten anything. My neighbour must have felt hungry too. He lifted his head again and said: "Don't expect any food from them. They're going to keep us hungry—on purpose! It will make us weak and vulnerable, you see ... and therefore too weak to escape. They'll only begin feeding us when it comes to labour. And that will make us compliant. Food for hard work; food as a means of control."

"Well, they've got to feed us with something if they want us to stay alive," I replied. I imagined how lovely it would be to bite into a chunk of bread, an apple, some cheese. I exhaled, exhausted.

"Yeah, yeah. They'll feed us some old, dry bread. But only enough to keep us alive," he answered.

It was now completely dark. The only flicker of light came from the dying embers and the torch which occasionally broke through the black surroundings. The man with the torch returned again. This time he shone the light directly in our faces, as if to examine each one of us, and then he did the same with the other group which included Durwyn. What or who was he looking for? His own face wasn't visible, now that it was completely dark, and the torch shed its light away from him.

Then another man began shouting: "Move, move…!" We got up, our bones stiff from sitting for hours. My muscles hurt all down my back and legs.

"They'll put us somewhere for the night. It's too dark and too late to leave now…" the villager close to me mumbled. "Come sunrise, it's all over. Our fate will be sealed. We'll be leaving our country, forever." I didn't answer him. What hope could I give, if there was none?

The Viking forced us to march us to a fishing hut next to the camp. Our feet were still chained together, to prevent anyone from escaping. Now at least we had a roof over our heads, and the wooden plank walls of the hut kept most of the wind out. But it was cold. No one lit a fire for us to keep us warm. We were left on the bare ground, without straw and skins. All we could do was lean back to back to keep warm. The Viking with the torch left the hut and closed the door. Darkness wrapped around us.

The few monks that were captured with us began to pray. They mumbled the Lord's Prayer, followed by more prayers in Latin. They repeated them over and over again.

"How does praying help now?" asked the villager who had spoken to me before. "It's a bit too late for that!"

"Oh, can't you just hold your mouth," someone else replied. "At least the monks are spreading some peace in this hopeless situation. It's better than complaining!"

"Yes, let them pray for those who have died today. Leave them in peace and stop ranting," another man said.

"Can prayer raise the dead, eh?" the first one carried on. "We've lost half a dozen men and half a dozen monks. It's all down to weapons! We weren't armed enough!"

"Quiet!" bellowed a guard from outside the hut, ending the argument.

Some of the villagers joined in the prayer, in low voices.

Outside seemed silent, and I wondered where all the Vikings, apart from those guarding us, stayed overnight. I had seen a deserted village close by. All the inhabitants must have left for fear of the Vikings, if they weren't already captured or killed. The Vikings might have gone there for the night, I concluded. They'd probably eat the provisions they found there, then lie in snug fur beds, next to the hearth.

Few words were exchanged during our imprisonment. If anyone did speak, they'd mumble a few words to the one next to them, until there was nothing more to be said and each of us suffered on in silence.

I wrapped my arms around my knees, trying to keep warm, and buried my head in my arms. With eyes closed I let the images of the day pass through my head. I was afraid of leaving the country. "Veronica," I whispered. My eyes filled with tears. Would we be separated for ever? Why had we met, only to be ripped apart again? I thought of Rohanna and Durwyn, who had just started their married life. How could Rohanna cope with another separation? Who would be there to console all the women left without husbands, the children without fathers? We were around twelve captured men here. But how many more had been caught? While thinking, I heard others begin to snore. I was tired and exhausted, but I couldn't manage to sleep.

Chapter Thirty-One—Change of Direction

I didn't remember falling asleep. Only when I woke with a jolt did I realise that I must have nodded off for an hour or so. I hoped that the events of the evening before were nothing but a bad dream. But within seconds I remembered everything. The nightmare was real; it hadn't ended. In fact, soon the worst part was likely to happen. We would leave Mercia and all that was dear to us. I closed my eyes, wishing this had never happened.

I heard voices outside the hut. Two men—probably the guard and someone else—were discussing something. I picked up bits of what they said. They were about to order us to go on board. One of the men seemed to insist that we should go on another boat than originally planned. He kept repeating it until the guard was convinced. Then there was a rattling at the door as the chain was unlocked.

Daylight slanted into the dark hut. I blinked, dazzled by the sudden light. Fresh air surged in; outside looked sunny and slightly windy—the right weather for travelling on water.

The guard chained our feet in a way that we could walk again.

The other man he had been talking to before now stood a few metres away, waiting for the two groups of prisoners to approach. He was wearing a hooded cloak, his back turned towards us as he looked down to the river, examining the conditions. The guard ushered us to him, and he then took over the lead. With a wave of his hand, he beckoned us to follow. He marched ahead, always remaining at a distance.

First we headed towards the river bank where the boats were waiting. Some men were already loading them with goods and pulling on ropes or adjusting rudders ready for departure. We slowly passed each boat, as if our leader could not decide which boat to go on. As we reached the last one, I expected him to order us to go aboard. My heart began to thump loudly and something deep inside me revolted. I didn't want to leave… I began to tug on the chain with my feet. I needed to get out of here, run away! The chains rattled around my ankles. They didn't allow more than half a step forward. I was chained to a man behind me and a man in front, and all of us were chained in a row. There was no option. I was a lamb brought to slaughter. I kept my head down in despair, like the rest of us.

Then suddenly the man who'd led us down here stretched out his arm, pointing in another direction and beckoning us to follow him. The river bank just here rose steeply from where the last boat was tied. The slope was covered in tall reeds with bushy heads like large paintbrushes.

Now everything happened very fast. Our leader exchanged a few words with the man who had guarded the fishing hut through the night—he must have been drowsy from too little sleep. He stared for a brief moment at the boats, then made his way back towards the fishing hut. Our leader, now in charge of us, beckoned us to come close, while hiding his face. When we were crowded together, he turned around and for the first time I saw his face.

"Ljot!" I called out in surprise. "How…?"

"No time for words," he answered. He bent down and undid our chains with shaking hands. My ankles were covered with red marks from the metal which had been rubbing against my skin for a day and a night. "Take off your footwear and carry it!" Ljot demanded. Then he pointed to the slope covered in reeds. "Quick, all of ye, get over there!"

Suddenly, it all made sense. Ljot was the man with the torch who had examined both groups of prisoners the night before. He had hidden his own face because he didn't want any of us to give away that we knew him! If someone had spoken his name out loud, it would have exposed his plan to help us escape, and the consequences would have been disastrous.

A dozen men now had to get out of sight fast, without attracting attention.

We crawled up the slope, huddled like beetles escaping a bird of prey, until we were out of sight of the Vikings on the river bank. The reeds enveloped us, like a mother hiding her child under her mantle. The ground was cold and sludgy and our bare feet were soon covered in black mud. The reeds scraped our hands and feet, as we constantly pushed stalks aside or stomped them down with our feet. We stopped to catch breath. I bent down and stroked the chain marks on my ankles. But Ljot urged us on.

"We need to keep going!" he said. "If they notice someone's missing, we need to be far enough so they can't catch up!"

Realising how serious our situation was, that this was our last chance of escaping a life of slavery in exile, we didn't ask any more. With the little strength that was left, I began to run. The prospect of freedom empowered me. During our run, a warbler or a duck occasionally flew up, surprised by us crossing their domain. We didn't dare to stop, even when out of breath. The reeds ended and we followed a narrow path that skirted the edge of the moor. Further up, along a smooth hill covered in grass and hedges, ran a wider cobbled path, or perhaps you could call it a road.

"We won't take the main road," Ljot announced. "It's too risky." The other men agreed.

"Of course," one of them replied, "the Roman road will be the first place where they'd try to hunt us down…"

"If they ever do try…" Ljot added. "The further away we are, the less likely they'll come after us. They want to sail east, remember, and right now the weather is good."

I breathed in the fresh air, filled with the scent of damp leaves. Never had I cherished freedom as much as I did now.

As we walked in silence, there was just the sound of many feet crunching on the gravel. We were hungry and exhausted after scrambling through the reeds. As the narrow path continued through bushes, we felt safer and carried on walking at a moderate pace. Blackberry and hazel bushes lined the path on both sides, when Ljot slowed down and suddenly stopped. At first I didn't understand why he was halting here. Then he crouched down by a cross made out of two thin sticks, stuck in the ground. You would hardly have noticed it when passing by. Behind the stick, hidden beneath thorny twigs, was a large leather bag. He dragged it out from its hiding place, opened it and revealed the contents: wrapped in a towel were enough flat breads and chunks of hard cheese to feed the whole group, with skin bottles filled with mead and water. We sat down on the path and enjoyed what seemed like the best meal ever.

After eating we had regained strength, and everyone began to talk and ask questions. Since the path was so narrow, most of us were sitting behind one another, and the group of escapees reached quite far back.

"Ljot, how did you manage this?" one of the villagers asked. "I mean, without causing any suspicion?"

"Well, as ye all know, I speak Norse language," he replied. (His English was now fluent, although in a Nordic accent with a rolling "r"). "My grandparents are from the same region as where these warriors are from, and I know the place they were planning to return to. I pretended that I had travelled with them from Norseland. Nobody noticed, since they are around 200 men and they couldn't know everyone. I pretended to be one of them."

"How did you make the guard believe that we must follow you?"

"I pretended that 'our' master had ordered the two groups of prisoners to go on the last boat, because the original ones were filled with wares and too laden to carry more passengers. The weight would make the ship sink if water got in during a storm, I explained.

"At first the guard was confused. He was meant to bring you all to one of the first boats. But I spoke convincingly, and he eventually believed me. I sent him back to his own master. 'If your master asks about the captives,' I told him, 'say they're all safely on the last ship.' But he didn't really care—he was just following orders."

"But you even managed to lead us away from the river bank, into the reeds…"

"Yes, this was the last but most important part of the plan. It could have cost our lives if it had gone wrong. If someone had seen us leaving the river bank, I was prepared to say that I had ordered ye all to go to the loo before departure."

"So *you* were the one with the torch examining boats and groups yesterday night!" another villager exclaimed.

"Yes, I had to make sure which group you were in, and check it would make sense to those I was tricking."

"A great trickster, you are…" one of the men shouted, patting Ljot on the back. "Well done!"

"We all decided I would be the best fit for this job since I hadn't been to the battle at the monastery. My wife told me not to leave, as Olfi wasn't well. So none of the raiders had seen me before. If I had fought alongside you, one or the other might have recognised me later at the river."

"How did you find out where we were and what had happened?" Durwyn asked.

"Bard, his sons and Karl had come back to our village with the terrible news that we had lost, that several were dead and others captured. We knew what that meant. We've seen slavery in my homeland—captives coming from different parts of the world. They have no chance of return; they own nothing, apart from their own body. They work hard without payment and eat little—a life of constant hardship and maltreatment." Ljot stretched his legs on the gravel. "And then ... all your women and children you'd leave behind." There was a silence in the air. "We needed to work out a plan fast," Ljot continued. "The Vikings would recognise Bard and the others, because they had been fighting against them. But they wouldn't know me. None of the warriors had seen me. We knew that raiders come in large numbers, so we hoped I could just mingle in the crowd and be disguised as one of them. So you see—I was everyone's last hope!"

"But what if they still find out and come after us?" a villager asked.

"They are eager to leave Mercia," Ljot replied. "They can't afford to waste time. I hope the escape will go unnoticed until they're already at sea. It's the weather they're following: missing the right moment could result in waiting for days or weeks—wasting time, food and energy ... getting irritated and bored. These men want to get going and bring their loot home."

We welcomed Ljot's narrative, but I was worried that the Vikings would return to Mercia—if not the same ones, then another group. But I kept these worries to myself.

After lunch, everyone felt refreshed and merry and we were eager to get back home. And when I say home, I meant home! Home was my wife, our friends, the village, Mercia. Durwyn's village had become my home. Home was where the people I cared for could be found. Each time the monks recited their prayers on the way home, I secretly joined in. Every time I thanked God for having sent Ljot and for all the coincidences that saved us.

Back in the village, we were greeted with tears of relief and endless hugs. If events had turned out differently, we could have been gone forever. We could have been killed in battle, drowned at sea or caught up in slavery for the rest of our lives. But instead we were back! Back in the small village, in Anglo-Saxon Mercia.

The monks split off on the way back to the village. Their path led back to the demolished monastery. I could only imagine how hard it must be for them to return to an abandoned monastery with their leader killed. As I watched them go, I felt gratitude towards the monks. I remembered their silent endurance, their trust and their prayers. Perhaps it was all down to their prayers that we were rescued.

There was a sad undertaking that had to be completed in the coming days. Bede and all the other monks who had been brutally killed needed to be buried. The funeral took place the following Sunday. Seven remaining monks led the mourning procession from the chapel to the graveyard behind the monastery. Singing and praying, they carried a cross in front, Bede's coffin in the middle of the procession, followed by six other coffins. Villagers came from near and far. Father Bede lay in a plain wooden coffin, no different from his fellow martyrs'. I watched with a heavy heart as his coffin was lowered into a cavity in the ground. One of the monks shovelled in soil until it was completely covered. The monks kneeled at the grave, while one of them sprinkled blessed water. They prayed with their heads bowed.

Villagers from all around came to help build and repair the monastery. People donated metal, gold and silver, copper and wood, and craftsmen made decorated crosses and Bible book covers. After a few weeks the monks took up copy-writing the Bible and illuminating the decorative letters again. They kept the garden, grew herbs, fruits and berries, and vegetables, baked bread and taught the faith.

Yet something important was still missing. The congregation had no leader, no prior. Who was going to replace Father Bede?

Chapter Thirty-Two—The New Prior

In late autumn, two of the monks, as well as Durwyn and I, gathered in Halig's small hut. We sat on the bench and enjoyed the warmth coming from the flickering fire in the hearth.

Halig still lived in his hermitage, although he was never completely alone, as people often came to seek his advice.

We drank hot tea from the pot resting on a heated stone by the hearth. A cold wind was blowing outside, heralding winter, but I felt warm and snug in my fur trousers and two layers under my fur tunic. The small hut was easy to heat: the warmth from the fire spread over our limbs, and the hot drink warmed us from inside.

"It's good to see you back, God bless you," Halig said, his small blue eyes sparkling. His grey beard might have grown a little longer in the past few years, and his bald patch a little broader.

"Well, thanks to Ljot for rescuing us," I said.

"Oh yes," Halig nodded and chuckled. "But what I meant is *your* safe return from the other side. You know…" Then I understood that he was glad that I was back in Mercia, from the other world.

"Yes, I'm glad to be back. And so is my wife…" I said, grasping my mug with both hands.

"God is good!" he said, his cheeks glowing red. "He makes impossible things possible!"

He poured more of the hot brew into our cups. And with a lower voice he asked me: "How is she? When is the child due?"

I was surprised that he already knew that Veronica was expecting our first baby. I put my cup back down without taking a sip. I remembered how Halig knew things without anyone having told him before. He had known that I was chosen to fight Ethón before he had even met me. And when I had turned up in his hut for the first time, he knew who I was—or at least that I was the one who was destined to fight the dragon. I cleared my throat. "Yes … she's doing well, apart from feeling sick sometimes. But there's still seven months to go…" I answered.

"Wonderful, wonderful," he answered with a smile. "Your wife will be blessed with more children… God is generous. As for you, my son," he continued, pointing at my chest, "you will never return to the other world."

I shuddered. Even though I never wanted to go back, Halig was now confirming that I'd never return.

Then one of the monks stood up. "Brother Halig," he said, "we need a replacement for Father Bede (may he rest in peace)." Before he continued, he made a sign of the cross and the others did so too. "We have thought long and hard, we have prayed and drawn lots. But we have come to the conclusion that none of us remaining monks is suitable as a leader. So now we have come to ask for you to become our new prior!"

Halig stood up to take care of the fire. He added water to the cauldron and then sat down, remaining quiet for a minute, contemplating the words spoken. He didn't smile and his face was unusually earnest. Perhaps he didn't want to leave his hermitage, this life of solitude, so close to nature and so close to God. He must have loved it that way. He had been living like this for many years. Why should he give it up? The monks would have to return to the monastery without a solution to their problem.

Then Halig cleared his throat and said: "Yes, I am ready. It is time for me to leave my hermitage. God's call is my command!"

"Does this mean we will soon welcome you as our new prior?" one of the monks asked, standing up.

"What else can I do?" Halig answered. "To do God's will is always best!"

"Praised be God!" the other monk said. "We are grateful, Halig … or may I say *Father* Halig!"

The others laughed and Halig smiled in return, a twinkle in his eye. "You'd better begin praying for me. I hope I will be a reason for praising God!"

Durwyn sat opposite me; there was a worried expression on his face. Halig asked him: "What are you worried about?"

Durwyn shrugged his shoulders, then said: "I was thinking about the losses from the Viking attacks."

"Yes," one of the monks agreed. "It took a lot of effort to restore the monastery, to put it back in shape."

Durwyn nodded. There was something else weighing on him.

"So?" Halig asked, raising his eyebrows. "Is that all?"

Durwyn sighed and then burst out: "What if they come again? What if the attacks are repeated? Won't we get weaker if we lose more men and material?"

I lowered my eyes. From history, I knew that at some point the Vikings would gain the upper hand in Mercia—in fact, the whole of Mercia would fall to them. But what should I say? Mentioning this wouldn't encourage anyone.

"My dear fellow men," Halig said, "this kingdom on earth is not comparable with the kingdom of Heaven. One will stay forever, and the other is only temporary. Like all things earthly, Mercia will not remain for ever. Long live our king and our people. But there are powers that are stronger than us: even if we unite to combine our strength, the invasions from outside are more powerful. If the

Vikings return, they will probably want to stay. Our land is fruitful, green and pleasant, and they will override us."

"But how could they? It is our land!" a villager exclaimed.

"Don't you think we have a better place to inherit than this world? Our true home is in Heaven, and that's the goal. Nothing on earth can replace our true home."

One of the monks nodded in agreement.

"But," Halig continued, smoothing his beard, "I have some good news: the Vikings will never return to destroy our monastery again."

"How? How can you tell?" Durwyn asked.

"A few nights ago," Halig began, "when I was lying in bed, preparing to fall asleep, Mary, herself, our Lord's Mother, appeared to me."

Everyone fell silent as Halig continued: "At first, I thought I was dreaming. But I wasn't. She stood there, at the foot of my bed, surrounded by a magnificent light. I sat up instantly, wondering if the time had arrived for me to leave this world." Halig took a sip from his mug.

"Were you afraid?" one of the villagers asked.

"Afraid? Maybe that's not right word. Perhaps a little nervous. But before I asked if she'd come to gather me to her, the Blessed Mary said: 'You will soon leave, my son!' and now I was quite sure my time was up and I was going to die. 'May I prepare myself?' I asked, hoping to say a couple of prayers for repentance and gratitude. She shook her head and smiled—and her smile was the most beautiful smile I have ever seen. 'No, she said. you are not yet to leave this world. You are going to leave your hermitage and go back to the monastery. You are needed there!' 'I see,' I replied, and then I understood that my time as a hermit was over. Just like Durwyn, I worried that the Vikings would attack us over and over again. And as if she could read my thoughts, Mother Mary said: 'There will be no more attacks on your monastery. You can rest assured. Father Bede's and my prayers of protection are upon your sanctuary.' 'Father Bede is with you in Heaven?' I asked, surprised. She nodded and smiled."

"So, what do you think about that?" Halig asked, after a pause. "We have our own saint in Heaven!"
There was gasping and one of the monks called out: "To know that Father Bede is in heaven is the greatest news since his death!"
"Finally, she blessed me in the name of her Son," Halig continued, "and then she disappeared before I could say thank you. The light had gone with Her and everything was dark and looked again like before, as if she had never appeared. But in my heart I felt immense joy." Halig's eyes shone.

Chapter Thirty-Three—Conclusion

As I finish telling my story, the logs in the fire are glowing. With the bellows I pump air into the charred wood, and the newly kindled flames leap up greedily. These logs will last for at least another hour. The light from the fire in our hearth illuminates the faces of those gathered near me: Veronica and our children, Wilfrid, Hilda and Godwin. Wilfrid, our first born, is as old as I was when I first came to Mercia; Hilda was born a year after him; and Godwin, our nestling, was born ten years after Hilda.

My cheeks are warm from the heat radiating from the flames. I am glad we have this source of heat, as the weather is icy. But this fire will always keep our home warm. I also feel warmth from within, as I count the blessings I have received.

Wilfrid rests his head on his knees and Hilda observes the flickering flames. The baby is wrapped in a blanket, his round face enclosed in a knitted hat tied under his chin. Baby Godwin heard my voice as I was telling my story, but he won't remember any of it. Sometime later in his life I will tell it again, and then it will remain in his heart and live on through him. It's the same narration I tell next day in the hall, where the people of our village are gathered.

In the hall I meet my sister Rohanna and Durwyn. The hall is crowded with villagers. Our children and their four children are sitting with the other village children on animal skins, playing games or resting. To mark the end of the narration, I twang some final notes on the lyre, the instrument I have inherited from the storyteller before me. The villagers remain quiet. Then after a minute's silence, one of the musicians picks up a leather drum and begins beating it gently with the padded end of a stick. The soft rhythm sounds like heartbeat. Another musician begins to sing, and more and more villagers join in.

The music brings back memories of the journey from Norway, when our Viking friends were singing and playing drums on the longboat. I think of Karl, Bjorn and Erik. They never went back to the monastery in Wales; instead they all entered the monastery in Hamberton, which now has as many monks as there used to be, before the Viking attack. Halig has proved to be right: the Vikings have never attacked us again. We must have been under special protection, because Viking raids still took place in other areas of Mercia. Halig was prior of the Hamberton monastery for over ten years, then found his final home when he died two years ago. Bard and his wife have stayed here in Durwyn's village, and have now reached old age. Over time they managed to accept their sons' calling, in fact they both became Christians themselves.

After a while the villagers' singing turns into humming, like the soft lilt of a lullaby. The night has progressed, and we will soon leave the warm longhouse and return to our homes.

Out in the open, the icy air almost cuts off our breath. The thatched roofs of our huts are covered with snow, and icicles decorate the entrances where the water has been dripping during the day. The snow-covered path leading to our hut has been trodden flat with footprints of the villagers returning to their homes. The frozen snow crunches under our feet. Clouds scurry past the moon, its light reflecting occasionally on the white landscape. We hug our woollen cloaks around us, and clouds of vapour emerge from our open mouths.

Wilfrid runs ahead as he usually does—always on the run. But then he slows down and waits for me to catch up so that he can walk next to me. I slow down my walking pace, because I know he wants to talk to me.

"Do you think the world you left behind is still the same, or do think it has changed a lot?" he asks.

I think for a moment. It's been many years since I left. I am now over forty years old—but who knows what time has passed there?

"I don't know," I answer. "I have left the other world for good. I will not go back. You know, strange as it sounds, I was already an old person back there… This here is now the life I'm focusing on—here and now. Here is my family, here is my home."

"I know," Wilfrid answers, but something keeps him going.

"When you came to Mercia as a child, the people needed your help. What if the people in that other world need our help right now?"

I stop walking. We watch our white breath puff into the air and fade away. Hilda is catching up from behind us.

"What gives you the idea they'd need our help?" I ask, wondering why he's suddenly so concerned. I look at his young face, which combines features from Veronica and me: the smooth elegance inherited from Veronica, and the reserved yet curious eyes like mine, which together make him unique. "It's not in our power to go to other worlds, you see," I carry on. "Rohanna and I were drawn into this world in a mysterious way. We couldn't have got here by ourselves."

Hilda has caught up, stops and listens to our talk. Why hasn't she run off with her friends or accompanied Veronica and baby Godwin into our warm hut? Her long thick hair spreads out on her shoulders from under her thick woven veil, tied around her slightly roundish face.

"I don't know exactly, it's just such a strong feeling," Wilfrid continues. "It's as if I *know* they need help, even though nobody's told me," he says. Hilda nods as if she understands what Wilfrid is talking about.

"Yes, I think so too," Hilda adds. "Someone *has* to go there!" She looks up to me with her brows pulled together, her eyes serious. I understand that she's not joking; she means what she says.

"Why? What is this all about?" I ask, perplexed.

And then we hear it. The three of us stand still on the frozen ground. The sky is black and has opened up to glinting stars. We turn around and glance across at the dark landscape. No one else seems to notice what makes our ears prick up. The crunching of feet on the hard snow has stopped. The last villagers in front of us disappear into their huts. We are left behind in the cold with no other sound than this: the sweet sound of a ringing bell coming from the chapel on the hill beyond the village.